D0955261

The
Transformative
CEO

The
Transformative
CEO

Impact Lessons from
Industry Game Changers

JEFFREY J. FOX
ROBERT REISS

NEW YORK CHICAGO SAN FRANCISCO
LISBON LONDON MADRID MEXICO CITY MILAN
NEW DELHI SAN JUAN SEOUL SINGAPORE
SYDNEY TORONTO

Copyright ©2012 by Jeffrey J. Fox and Robert Reiss. All rights reserved. Printed in the United States of America. Except as permitted under the United States Copyright Act of 1976, no part of this publication may be reproduced or distributed in any form or by any means, or stored in a database or retrieval system, without the prior written permission of the publisher.

1 2 3 4 5 6 7 8 9 0   DOC/DOC   1 0 9 8 7 6 5 4 3 2

ISBN: 978-0-07-179498-5
MHID: 0-07-179498-0

e-book ISBN: 978-0-07-179499-2
e-book MHID: 0-07-179499-9

Design by Mauna Eichner and Lee Fukui

McGraw-Hill books are available at special quantity discounts to use as premiums and sales promotions, or for use in corporate training programs. To contact a representative, please e-mail us at bulksales@mcgraw-hill.com.

This book is printed on acid-free paper.

Contents

Acknowledgments

Doris Michaels and Pauline Hsia, DSM Literary Agency, in New York City for continued professional representation.

Delia Berrigan Fakis, Editorial Strategist, Hallmark Gift Books.

Thanks to the McGraw-Hill team for making this book happen.

Erin, Elizabeth Cosette Communications and Public Relations, LLC in Avon, Connecticut for tirelessly keeping this project on track.

And a special thanks to each Transformative CEO involved in this initiative, which essentially defines a new leadership category. Each contributor was courteous, modest, inspiring, and provided deep thinking and stunning business and life wisdom. Your de vivo endorsement of this book is . . . transformative.

Authors' Notes

In college I read Napoleon Hill's classic *Think and Grow Rich*. The premise was unique: in 1908 Andrew Carnegie, a leading industrialist of his era, introduced the young Napoleon Hill to the world's most successful business people so Hill could write a book about what set these people apart. I thought Napoleon Hill had the world's best job, and I secretly dreamed that I might one day have such an opportunity.

Years later, after being a strategy consultant for CEOs and having read over 500 business books, I came to realize that certain top CEOs had unique abilities to build businesses, create jobs and achieve success. That was the genesis of "The CEO Show," where I've used radio as the channel to help CEOs share their insights on business and personal success. From the beginning, I had a higher purpose of disseminating CEO wisdom ... realizing by reaching enough people I could do my small part to elevate individuals, business, the economy, even the world. Though it didn't initially dawn on me, I had come full circle and was actually living my dream.

Now that "The CEO Show" has passed its fifth anniversary, and after interviewing over 250 top CEOs, it is clear that the exceptional CEOs share one common trait: they are transformative. They know how to revitalize a company, reinvent an industry, and sometimes even reboot society. In *The Transformative CEO*—which I believe defines a new category of leadership—Jeffrey and I were able to distill the CEOs' wisdom into a few vital lessons, each of which will make you more of a game changer and successful driver of transformation. May this book help you in your career and in your life.

ROBERT REISS

How often do you get the chance to have super-high-performing CEOs talk directly to you? To tell you how they think, how they decide, their management principles? Their secret success sauce recipes? How cool is it to sit across the table from the guy who hired a Duck to be his company spokesperson, or the woman who resuscitated Howard Hughes' helicopter company? Been homeless? Find out from John Paul DeJoria how to get over it. Ever been exiled, as a 10-year old, by Fidel Castro? Ralph de la Vega has been there. Want to meet CEOs who are friends with Spiderman, The Incredible Hulk, Frankie Valli and The Four Seasons, with your local UPS man, with the lady who delivers your birthday balloons?

If yes, read on.

JEFFREY FOX

Meet the Transformative CEOs

1-800-Flowers. Jim McCann, founder and CEO, created a new retail category becoming the largest florist and gift company in the world. His was the first company to use its 800 number both as a brand name and as a "store." In 1992, Jim McCann began selling over the Internet, one of the first companies to do so.

Aflac. Chairman and CEO Dan Amos is among the longest tenured CEOs in the Fortune 500. He helped transform a successful family business into a Fortune 125 company, and became an industry leader with revenues of more than $22 billion. Aflac is a perennial winner of numerous corporate awards. Dan Amos has accomplished much in his career, but is probably best known for introducing the Aflac Duck.

Air Canada. When Calin Rovinescu took over Air Canada as CEO in April 2009, the airline was approaching bankruptcy. Thirteen months later Air Canada was cited by Sky Trax as the number one airline in North America.

AT&T Mobility. At 10 years old, Ralph de la Vega was separated from his parents for 4 years. This experience ultimately taught Ralph the importance of overcoming obstacles. Ralph de la Vega is CEO, AT&T Mobility and oversees 46,000 employees, serving almost 100 million customers, with more than $50 billion in revenue. When Cingular Wireless merged with AT&T Wireless, he brought together two company cultures of 30,000 people each in just 19 days. He was instrumental in introducing the iPhone.

Beekley Corp. Ayn LaPlant has been CEO, or president, for 21 years. Beekley created a diagnostic marking system for radiologists to more accurately read mammograms and x-rays. Beekley's products have saved millions of women's lives.

Bicron Corporation. Chris Skomorowski, CEO, is transforming a sleepy 30-year old electronics maker into a global high-tech growth company.

Black Entertainment Television (BET). Robert L. Johnson is founder and chairman of The RLJ Companies, a diverse portfolio of companies. He was founder and chairman of Black Entertainment Television, the nation's first and leading television network providing quality programming for the African-American audience. In 2001, Robert Johnson sold BET to Viacom for approximately $3 billion.

Build-A-Bear Workshop. Maxine Clark, chief executive bear, founded the company in 1997, with a new retailing concept that enables customers to build a bear, or bring their stuffed animals to life. Build-A-Bear has over 400 stores, and is one of the world's most beloved companies.

Campbell Soup. When Doug Conant became CEO in 2001, Campbell Soup had lost half its market value in one year, and had actually stooped to reducing the amount of chicken in its signature chicken noodle soup. By transforming the culture first, he led Campbell Soup Company's turnaround.

Cirque du Soleil. Daniel Lamarre, CEO, transformed Cirque from offering seven "traditional" shows, to 22 innovative creations on five continents, including new genres such as "Love."

Coldwell Banker. Jim Gillespie is CEO of Coldwell Banker Real Estate LLC with over 86,000 global agents and employees. Since becoming CEO in 2004 Gillespie has had five different chief operating officers (COOs), four of whom have become CEOs of other major real estate firms.

Container Store. Kip Tindell is founder and CEO of The Container Store, the original storage and organization store. The Container Store is consistently selected as one of *Fortune* magazine's "100 Best Companies to Work For."

Danaher Corp. Larry Culp became CEO in 2001. During his tenure revenues have tripled to over $13 billion, and market capitalization has increased more than 400 percent to over $35 billion. Danaher cracked the code on how to acquire companies and seamlessly integrate them with accretive earnings and minimal fallout. The vaunted Danaher Business System is deployed globally to continuously eliminate unnecessary costs and waste from every process, function and operation in the corporation.

Eggland's Best. Charles Lanktree, CEO, led Eggland's Best to reinvent the ultimate commodity—the egg. This has resulted in dozens of taste and nutrition awards and sales growth of over 17 percent annually since 1995.

General Mills. Ken Powell, CEO, leads what is one of the world's great marketing companies, and is probably the most "volunteering" company in the world.

Girl Scouts. Kathy Cloninger led perhaps the largest restructure of a not-for-profit consolidating 315 offices into 112, realigning the entire organization, while marshalling 1 million volunteers.

Griffin Health Services Corporation. Patrick Charmel is CEO of a 160-bed community teaching hospital that is the flagship of an international network of customer centric health care facilities that have adopted the innovative Planetree model.

Home Depot. At 49 years old Bernie Marcus was fired from his last position, and without a job, he cofounded Home Depot. Bernie Marcus was CEO for 19 years, creating the modern American do-it-yourself society.

Honest Tea. Seth Goldman started this environmentally, socially conscious company without a clue as to the enormous challenges in the way of creating a national beverage brand.

ING DIRECT. Led by CEO and Chairman, Arkadi Kuhlmann, ING DIRECT opened for business in 2000. His vision was to "bring Americans back to savings." He established a new banking model that returned savings to customers. Within a decade, in a highly regulated industry ING DIRECT experienced unparalleled growth becoming the largest savings bank in America, with $90 billion in assets.

International Data Group (IDG). Patrick J. McGovern, founder and chairman of IDG, envisioned the future of technology and the need to share information, building the world's largest technology media company. Starting with *Computerworld* magazine, IDG has over 200 print titles, over 460 websites, and produces 700 technology events per year. IDG founded the Dummies book series. In 2000, Pat McGovern and his wife, Lore Harp McGovern, pledged $350 million to establish The McGovern Institute for Brain Research at MIT.

Paul Mitchell Systems. John Paul DeJoria went from being homeless to becoming a multibillionaire. He started several companies, including Paul Mitchell Systems and Patrón Spirits. He espouses a philosophy that corporations must lead the way in bettering society.

Kaiser Permanente. George Halvorson is chairman and CEO with responsibility for 37 hospitals, nearly 9 million members and 180,000 employees with more than $47 billion in revenue. Kaiser has created a new, integrated health care model that is changing the direction of healthcare by enhancing clinical outcomes while significantly reducing costs. Kaiser was cited as the number one diversified company in America in 2011.

Marvel Entertainment. Soon after Peter Cuneo became CEO of Marvel, its stock price hit a low of $.96 a share in 2000. With only $3 million in cash at one point, the company utilized Marvel's only asset: its unequaled IP catalogue of fantasy characters, such as Spiderman. By emphasizing major motion pictures, and by increasing its comic book market share, the company achieved rapid financial growth. In 2009, Disney purchased Marvel for $54 per share. Marvel was one of seven turnarounds Peter Cuneo engineered in his remarkable career.

McDonald's. Jim Skinner is CEO of McDonald's with responsibility for 33,000 restaurants and 1.7 million employees. When Jim Skinner took the helm, McDonald's stock price and food quality had stagnated. Jim Skinner turned around the company, resulting in nine straight years of organic growth.

Microcare Corp. Chris Jones, CEO, has transformed a one-man manufacturer's rep organization into the industry leader in precision cleaning of high-value industrial parts and components.

MTV International. Bill Roedy, first CEO of MTV International, started connecting MTV with the world. At the end of his tenure, MTV International was shown in 33 languages, in 162 countries, airing on 172 local TV channels reaching an audience of 2 billion people. Bill Roedy is a strong advocate of international social issues.

NetApp. Under Executive Chairman Dan Warmenhoven's leadership, NetApp pioneered a new model for data storage. NetApp went from incorporation to over $1 billion in revenues in under ten years. NetApp was rated by *Fortune* as the number one best company to work for in America in 2009.

Ogilvy & Mather. Chairman, Shelly Lazarus, has pioneered brand building via corporate philanthropy. She is also a board member of committee encouraging corporate philanthropy.

PAETEC. Arunas Chesonis is founder, CEO, and chairman of PAETEC. Started in 1998, PAETEC, a B2B communications company, became a Fortune 1000 company in 2010. This significant growth was fueled by a progressive company culture.

Panasonic. Joseph Taylor is CEO and chairman of Panasonic Corporation of North America. He is transforming the iconic B2C company into a B2B leader.

Patriarch Partners. Though few may know the name, Patriarch Partners is the largest female-owned business in America. Founder and CEO, Lynn Tilton, created a new business model with the mission of saving American jobs, and resurrecting American manufacturing. In the last decade, Patriarch has acquired more than 150 companies and in so doing has saved 250,000 jobs.

Regus. Mark Dixon is founder and CEO of Regus, a provider of innovative and flexible workplaces available for as little as $25 per month and is used by more than 1 million people in over a 100 countries. The founder of several other entities, his business philosophy is that recessions create significant business opportunities.

Ritz-Carlton. Simon Cooper is the former president of this quintessential "customer-first" company.

Royal Caribbean Cruises Ltd. Richard Fain has been chairman and CEO for over 23 years, and has led what most thought impossible in the cruise industry—building the world's largest ships with new, open center architecture featuring carousels, rock climbing, and even ice rinks.

Sodexo Health Care. Patrick Connolly, president, pioneered the model of nonclinical, unique care services in hospitals. Sodexo Health Care has 65,000 employees. Sodexo was cited as the number two diversified company in America.

TeleBrands. AJ Khubani, founder and CEO, created late night direct response television commercials. "As seen on TV," and "Wait there's more," have sold millions of popular inexpensive products.

UBS Paine Webber. Former chairman and CEO of UBS Paine Webber, Joe Grano merged the two companies in the largest, least disruptive combination of its time. He is now CEO, Centurion Holdings, and the producer of the Broadway hit m
usical *Jersey Boys*.

UPS. Scott Davis became CEO of UPS in 2007 just before the Great Recession. Utilizing growth strategies, bold investments, and aggressive restructuring, the 400,000 employee company emerged from the contraction in a stronger market share position.

Vanguard Group, Inc. After being fired, John Bogle revisited his college thesis and created Vanguard. Vanguard was a new financial service business model. Vanguard is the world's largest mutual fund organization, with assets over $1.7 trillion.

Walker & Dunlop Co. When Willy Walker joined as CEO in 2003, the multifamily financing firm had one office in Bethesda, Maryland, and was not ranked among the nation's large mortgage originators. By 2010, Willy Walker had grown the firm into the eleventh largest commercial real estate lender in the United States. Continuing the transformation of a small family-owned business into a national powerhouse, Willy Walker took Walker & Dunlop public on the NYSE in 2010.

Waste Management. David Steiner is CEO of this leading provider of waste reduction and environmental services. Waste Management has more than 20 million customers, and 43,000 employees. Those employees are leading Waste Management's strategy to transform "waste into value" and to someday eliminate landfills.

Xerox. During her tenure as CEO of Xerox from 2001 to 2009, Anne Mulcahy led the storied turnaround of Xerox Corporation. She shifted from saving Xerox to saving children as chairperson of Save the Children.

Zappos. At 24 years old, Tony Hsieh sold his first company, LinkExchange, to Microsoft for $265 million. He later became an investor and then CEO of Zappos, a small online shoe company with sales of $1.6 million. Through a revolutionary customer service model, a decade later Zappos had over $1 billion in gross merchandise sales and was acquired by Amazon. Today Zappos is widely cited as one of the world's most admired companies.

1

The Transformative CEO

The transformative CEO comes in all sizes, colors, ages, genders, ethnicities. He or she has a different style, personality, background, ability. It is what he or she accomplishes that distinguishes the transformative CEO from all the rest. The transformative CEO turns around companies, creates new industries, revolutionizes the way business is done, commercializes amazing products, changes society. The transformative CEO is obsessed with company culture, customers, innovation, and leadership.

The transformative CEO encourages risk taking, but prevents recklessness. He or she embraces mavericks, free-thinkers, outsiders, as long as they embrace the winning company culture. He or she woos, cajoles, leads her colleagues, but is not interested in winning a popularity contest. The transformative CEO sees opportunities where others see certain failure. The transformative CEO, according to Phil Griffin, president of MSNBC, "must see around the corner." The transformative CEO spots the right wave to ride, and then gets the organization to surf to success. The transformative CEO creates wealth, taxpayers, donations, job security, unlimited futures, grateful communities.

The transformative CEO changes or creates.

2

On Transformative CEOs

Arkadi Kuhlmann (CEO, ING DIRECT): "Never in history have the issues facing the CEO been more daunting and challenging than they are today. We are in a global marketplace. We can be constantly, instantly, visibly in touch with customers, colleagues, suppliers anywhere on the planet. Information, cash, credit, invoices, payments, data, bids, disinformation, rumors flow seamlessly around the world every second of every day. These forces shorten the business cycles. New products must get to markets faster. Competitive responses are faster. Markets occur, evolve, and devolve overnight. Given these immediate pressures, the CEO must align short-term investments and short-term results with long-term, over-the-horizon goals.

"A CEO's term of service keeps getting shorter. Time to build a transformative culture is shorter. Yet, the activities of a company, like multiplying organisms, keep getting more interwoven, more complex, more difficult to measure and manage.

"Our best CEOs will therefore be a rare breed of renaissance individuals: people equally comfortable with art and science, literature and math, Paris, Texas, and Paris, France, society and business. They are individuals who can simplify; who have experience-honed intuition, street smarts; are mentally fast, nimble, and above all, the best CEOs are creative.

"Blending such qualitative and quantitative disciplines is not easy, but it is demanded by the wide range of challenges in the new world. And the blending never stops: the CEO's continuous learning journey is indeed a steep mountain.

"For CEOs, there are countless stakeholders who will vote not once, but daily, relentlessly, remorsefully. They will vote at the cash register, at the annual meeting, in the boardroom, at the banker's office, on

LinkedIn and Twitter, and in social media ballot boxes still unimagined. 'Managing in a glass box,' will be literally true.

"Brave and resourceful, creative and effective, will be the hallmarks of the transformative CEO. For the transformative CEO has no choice but to change the game, and to change the game forever."

David Steiner (CEO, Waste Management): "We are transforming from an old-fashioned trash hauler business to an organization that is intent on turning waste into value, thereby, some day, eliminating dumps and landfills. Any time you are going through a transformation, you have to get the big things exactly right. And the biggest thing is to be sure you have the hearts and minds of employees. We want to save the planet. On this matter, our employees are way ahead of the game. I didn't have to win their hearts and minds, I joined them."

Larry Culp (CEO, Danaher Corp.): "Leaders must make sure the organization does not compromise on talent. Leaders must constantly help the company define 'great talent.' Our number one core value is 'The

Best Team Wins.' We firmly believe that if you have the right people, aligned on values, skills, competencies, then performance follows. With good people errors in strategy and execution will be limited and quickly corrected when they occur. When an organization has talent throughout, leaders can set the bar high, thoughtfully and fairly, and reset that bar continuously to drive great results."

Pat McGovern (Founder and Chairman, International Data Group [IDG]): "The transformative CEO is constantly in the marketplace meeting with customers and prospective customers. It is in the marketplace where one can spot emerging trends and unfilled customer needs. If you can fill the need with a profitable price, and that price is lower than the economic value delivered to the customer, then you have the rationale to form a business unit. To make the business successful find that person who will love the idea; who will enthusiastically engage customers; and who will hire similarly motivated people who will make it happen. Treat that leader as you would like to be treated: with trust and with frequent, public, visible appreciation."

Robert L. Johnson (Founding CEO, Black Entertainment Television, Founder and Chairman, The RLJ Companies): "The transformative CEO creates something so compelling it changes people's lives and becomes an iconic brand that sustains itself over time. This takes a visionary leader who can inspire talented people to build a company with a culture based on integrity and value creation. Building a company is like parenting a child: need to nurture, plus lots of love, including tough love."

Arunas Chesonis (CEO, PAETEC Corp.): "The transformative CEO must have no fear of failure. Even a bit of trepidation can demoralize colleagues, whose complete confidence in the mission is necessary to succeed. And leaders must have a 'no greed' credo. The team must feel there is a fair sharing of the wealth, the value, they are helping to create. To do otherwise will lose support of key colleagues."

Anne Mulcahy (CEO, Xerox [ret.]): "The main function of the CEO is to create followership. Having a great strategy, having a great execution plan is insufficient to be a good leader. It's about the CEO's ability to deploy, to be credible with your people, to clearly communicate. Followership and building super competent teams are the most important aspects of transformational leadership."

Daniel Lamarre (CEO, Cirque du Soleil): "In Cirque du Soleil's case, the transformation was taking this fabulously creative organization, which performed 7 'traditional' shows (traditional to Cirque) to a globally recognized entertainment business that now has 22 shows on 5 continents. Our lessons are: build on the fundamental values and company culture that keep us unique (which for us is mind-blowing creativity); diversify our performance format and content; preserve our stunning high-level acrobatics, theatricality, and original choreography. All presented with a dollop of the special Cirque du Soleil touch. Of course, this transformation must be executed with the complete knowledge and enthusiastic cooperation of all our people."

Mark Dixon (CEO, Regus): "The transformative CEO is a surfer. Business is a surfing experience. Ride great waves. Set up great businesses. Every ride (I've had eight) is exhilarating, exhausting, better than the one before. You need an alchemy of talented people, skills, ideas, relentless execution, sheer effort. Create a business that is respected by colleagues and customers. Surfing the wave of success, oxygen filling your lungs, is one of the special moments in the life of the CEO."

Jim McCann (CEO, 1-800-Flowers): "Everyone has setbacks. Transformative CEOs gets over them quicker, recover faster. They learn, adapt, dust themselves off, and get back to the job. Transformative CEOs focus on creating a culture; an environment where people have the opportunity to perform and grow. People want to do a good job. They want to be part of successful change, of constantly transforming."

George Halvorson (CEO, Kaiser Permanente): "Culture trumps strategy. Every CEO should manage the culture of the organization with great care. Culture engineering and culture management involves defining values and core beliefs, setting up basic rules and guidelines, communicating, and modeling. The CEO must be a visible model of the desired culture. What the CEO does and says sends the culture message.

The organization will understand. Culture and strategy must be intertwined. The job of the CEO is to ensure that the culture of the organization is such that the work gets done as desired."

John Bogle (Founding CEO, Vanguard Funds): "As to being a transformative leader, I have no idea. It takes a superman to transform an organization, and I'm no superman. And I started Vanguard de novo in 1974, so there was nothing to transform. I made my human values and investment strategies clear from the outset, and, I guess you could say, in a dictatorial fashion. Those values are our culture. Treat others, from the highest to the most humble, with the same kind of respect with which you would like to be treated; act with integrity, not just in words, but in deeds; work hard; be frugal, avoid waste and spend only on what you need. Our tiny crew, 28 people in the beginning, seemed to believe in those same values. To this day we pass these values along to all those crew members who have joined us, now 13,000 fine people."

Maxine Clark (Founder and CEO, Build-A-Bear Workshop): "If imagination is part of transformation, then we have transformed the way plush toys are sold. But it is primarily the imagination of our customers that drives our business. You must stay in touch with the customer, no matter how much you are alike with the customer, you are not your customer. You need to keep your world wide open to constantly stay in close touch with your customers to know what they are thinking."

Bill Roedy (Founding CEO, MTV International): "My feelings on the role of the CEO, on leadership, are shaped by my years at West Point, and then Vietnam. One leadership principle is, 'first on the battlefield, last to leave.' When building an entrepreneurial international business, there is a crisis, somewhere, every day. You have to be with your 'lieutenants' to help. And, have your feet on the soil. Be there. Get into the culture of your markets. My overriding philosophy for global brand and business building is to 'respect and reflect the local cultures.'"

How To Turn Around
a Company

Company turnarounds are needed because what once worked no longer does. Turnarounds are not easy; nine out of ten turnarounds fail. Here is how to successfully turn around a dying, stumbling company.

1. **Have a *vision* of what the new company can be; of where the company can go; and, most importantly, how to get there.** The vision need not be some mystical view of the future. A simple mission statement will do. During WWII, England's Prime Minister Winston Churchill told his brave Royal Air Force (RAF) pilots: "Bomb the bridges and get back safely by dawn." Be sure everyone understands the plan.

Peter Cuneo (CEO, Marvel Entertainment): "In an uncertain environment, people naturally look for leadership. They are looking for a vision. If you are honest with them and if you consistently walk the talk, the organization will start to believe."

Jim Skinner (CEO, McDonald's): "If you have vision, and a good business concept, then you can craft strategies and an action plan."

Lynn Tilton (CEO, Patriarch Partners): "Rebuilding a broken company takes a team of people with alignment of vision, passion, perseverance, and courage of conviction; willingness to walk in the darkness one foot in front of the other until they see the light."

John Paul DeJoria (Founding CEO Paul Mitchell Systems; Founder Patrón Spirits): "Our vision was to provide hair salons with the finest, most unique products they would use every day."

2. **Get the *culture* right.** Create a winning atmosphere. Make it perfectly clear what good performance means. Get rid of mediocrity. Get rid of constant doomsayers.

Be sure everyone understands the ethics of the company.

Peter Cuneo: "When managing a turnaround, 'average' is unacceptable. You have to change the culture from accepting and living with 'average' and 'good enough,' to one where excellence is the new benchmark."

Jim Skinner: "The leader must shift the culture, the employee mindset, from living with the status quo, to one that celebrates success. At McDonald's our culture is about commitment to execution, opportunity, and growth."

Lynn Tilton: "When we bought MD Helicopters it had been shuttered for three years, customer support was nonexistent, and the company was mired in a host of dire problems. Helicopters was the house that Howard Hughes built. Hughes embodied the 'rebel with a cause spirit,' working against the grain, battling against those who wanted to shut him down. Down deep that is still the MD culture. We rekindled the spirit, resurrected MD's great products, and repaired the customer support problem with haste. Today, the Howard Hughes legacy is wonderfully alive and will live on long into the future as well."

Doug Conant (CEO, Campbell Soup Company): "When I arrived, Campbell was in tough shape. The company had lost half its market value in one year. The shareholders and employees were deeply concerned. Sales were declining and morale was terrible. As one of my mentors would say, 'we were trapped in a circle of doom' . . . consistently over-promising and under-delivering. It was a toxic culture. I was brought in to rebuild the culture that had made Campbell Soup such an iconic company for 125 years."

3. **Get the *right* people.** The transformative CEO is like a professional sports team coach: always looking for the best athletes; putting the players in the right positions; making sure every player knows what to do to win. The transformative CEO knows the culture he or she wants, and hires and fires, in the context of that culture. If the CEO makes a hiring mistake, he or she admits it, and fixes the mistake.

Peter Cuneo: "To be successful you must convince others to join you and change the company's culture to one that reinforces your goals. It is all about hiring the right people. Fully, 90 percent of the effort in a turnaround is keeping people motivated."

Jim Skinner: "It is critical to get the right people in place to deliver. The right people in the right place at the right time. *If you are the smartest person in the room, then you are not getting the best advice.* And get diversity. If everyone looks like you and sounds like you, you are not getting the best advice. It is imperative that leaders listen to everyone."

Lynn Tilton: "I have learned through my failures and the failures of those around me, the drivers necessary to turn around a distressed company. The most important thing is the talent of the management team and the momentum they create to rise from the abyss."

Doug Conant: "It was clear for a host of reasons that the management team that was in place was not getting the job done. I set a simple performance bar: leaders were going to be evaluated on what they accomplished, and how they treated people with whom they worked. There were 350 people on the global leadership team. Ultimately, 300 did not meet expectations. We promoted 150 high-character, high-performance, well-respected people from within the organization and we recruited 150 like-minded leaders from other blue chip companies outside the organization. At the time, there were 20,000 people overall in the company and slowly but surely they saw we meant business and began to believe in our collective ability to effect a turnaround."

4. **Never forget the *customer*.** Turnarounds are rife with problems, many requiring urgent attention. It is easy to let the urgent drain focus from the important. *The single most important factor for business success is having a profitable customer.* The transformative CEO never lets the organization take its eyes off the customer.

> **Peter Cuneo:** "Ultimate business success is determined by the consumers, the customers who pay for your product or service because they are permanently, emotionally attached to your brands."

> **Jim Skinner:** "We wouldn't sell billions of hamburgers a year if we did not have millions of fantastic customers."

Lynn Tilton: "Every business strategy starts with the customers. The closer you can get to the customers the better your business will perform, because you will understand how the customers think and what they truly want and need."

Doug Conant: "There are two primary groups that need to be focused on in the turnaround of a consumer products company: the consumers of the company's products and the employees. The prior management, under enormous cost and earnings pressure, had compromised some of the products by cutting back on key ingredients while actually raising prices. Not surprisingly, sales began to slip. As sales slipped, advertising and promotion budgets were cut back to meet short term earnings goals. Without sufficient advertising and promotion support, sales continued to slip and trading relationships with our retail partners became strained. As trading tensions mounted, sales slipped even further, earnings growth became even more challenged and the company felt pressured to resort to layoffs given the lower sales base. The layoffs, however, also limited the company's ability to find new growth avenues which put further pressure on the company's growth profile. The first thing I did was talk frankly and honestly with all of the stakeholders. We then put a three year Transformation Plan in place to make the company competitive again—getting the right leadership in place, establishing the right standards and disciplines, improving product quality, restoring the advertising and promotion budgets to competitive levels, streamlining the portfolio, and improving the work life of our employees."

5. **Write a one-page action plan that a 10-year old can understand.** A turnaround plan, or any business or marketing plan that can fit in a shirt pocket gets executed. Those cliché-filled, business-jargon filled, neatly packaged plans are exercises in futility. The action plan must not contain even a pinch of nuance. If something is open to interpretation, it will always be interpreted, and it will be interpreted differently than intended. The action plan must galvanize, direct, inform, and motivate everyone in the organization.

Peter Cuneo: "Our plan was simple to understand, but far more difficult to execute. We had to radically change the way Marvel had been run. The key elements in this transformation included:

- Re-engaging with comic book readers by vastly improving the quality of our efforts in story creation and illustration.

- Reintroducing Spiderman, The Incredible Hulk, Ironman, and others among our 7,000 fantasy characters to a global audience through big budget motion pictures.

- Adopting a frugal view of every operation in the company to conserve cash.

- Creating a licensing business model that did not require capital contributions from Marvel.

- Make it fun to come to work every day."

Jim Skinner: "The key to our turnaround was removing distractions. Our plan could have been titled 'Back to Basics'. This was the plan:

- Sell off Chipotle, along with other non-McDonald's restaurants and businesses.

- Redirect all talent and energy into the McDonald's brand and business.

- Ratchet up our attention and energy into our relationships with our terrific franchisees.

- Serve delicious food when our customers want it.

To keep us on track, whenever an idea comes up that might be even mildly distractive I ask, 'How does this help the hamburger business?' which, of course, is a metaphor for, 'How does this help McDonald's?' Back to basics has resulted in nine straight years of same store sales growth."

Lynn Tilton: "This was our plan to turn around MD Helicopters

- Start reliving the Howard Hughes's "rebel with a cause" mission.

- Start selling. MD makes the fastest, quietest helicopter in the world. Customers love it. Sell it.

- Rebuild reputation via performance.

- Dramatically improve customer support, including on-time delivery of parts that work.

We went from zero sales to more than $200 million and were profitable. Today, no one questions if MD is here to stay."

Doug Conant: "I have a foundational belief that the first place you have to win is with the people who do all the work. You have to do what you promise. You have to truly value someone as a person, not as some name on a chart. And you have to give the consumer what she wants. And if you don't tell 'em, you won't sell 'em.

"Those ideas were the basis for our Campbell Soup Company turnaround.

- First day on the job: promise the employees that we value them, and that they should judge us against that principle.

- Fix up the facilities. Make people proud to work at Campbell Soup."

Doug Conant: "The company is anchored in Camden, New Jersey . . . one of the poorest and most dangerous cities in the United States. In a city of roughly 78,000 people, there are 30-40 murders per year.

Over time, our World Headquarters facility in Camden had become a fortress to help our employees feel safe. It had morphed into what looked like a minimum security prison. As a result, it was replete with high fences topped with razor wire and guard towers. It seemed to me that we had to change the facility if we were seriously committed to changing the culture. We replaced the high fences and razor wire with attractive estate fencing. We spruced up the campus wherever we could with fresh paint and greenery. We professionalized our security staff and procedures. Ultimately, we dramatically upgraded the entire campus with state of the art facilities and first class amenities.

- Upgraded the culture with new leadership that brought a winning attitude to work every day and did not tolerate abusiveness, unfairness or discrimination in the workplace in any way, shape or form. We focused on valuing the people in our organization with the intention of inspiring them to value our agenda as a company.

- Upgraded products to be best of class.

- Reinvested in advertising and promotion to rebuild our brand equities with consumers.

- Stepped-up innovation to better meet consumer needs.

- Carefully monitored employee engagement with a highly regarded independent survey, recognizing that it was the critical success factor for engineering an effective turnaround. Over time, employee engagement went from being among the worst in the Fortune 500, to being among the best with 17 people highly engaged in their work for every one person who is not. Among our top 350 global leaders, the ratio is over 70 to one."

Successful turnarounds have certain things in common: bold missions, simple plans, clear-cut culture, good talent, diligent execution. The same rules apply to transforming a brand, a factory, a team, a business unit.

Play by these rules.

4

Protect or Change the Company Culture

Defining "corporate culture" is like defining artwork or country music. Some forgotten philosopher at one time helpfully quipped, "If it sounds like country, then it's country." For that insight, the world is forever grateful. Or when it comes to artwork, one can turn to Supreme Court Justice Potter Stewart who clarifyingly proclaimed, "I know art, and this is not that."

There are oodles of scholarly articles and papers trying to characterize and capture the notion of "corporate culture." Perhaps the definitive work is Dr. Larry Senn's,

"Organizational Character as a Methodological Tool," published in 1969.

Corporate culture is a company's personality.

There is no wrong or right corporate culture. There is no good or bad corporate culture. There are only winning and losing corporate cultures.

> **Tony Hsieh (CEO, Zappos):** "For any company, the kind of culture they have doesn't really matter. What matters, what's important, is that it is a strong culture, and that it is consistent throughout the entire company."

If the company is successful, and has been for some time, then the CEO must nurture and protect that culture, the company personality. If the company is failing, and has been failing for far too long, then the new transformative CEO, whether from the outside or a company insider, must immediately craft a plan to implement a winning culture.

Step one in transforming a company culture is for the CEO to get a change-it mandate from the Board, or the owners, or the leaders, or from whomever is running the show.

Step two for the CEO recruited from the outside is
to spend the first 100 days

- Looking into every nook of the company.

- Meeting and listening to as many employees as
  possible, at every rank and level, and especially
  listening to those people making and selling
  things.

- Meet all important customers.

- Meet all critical suppliers.

- Ask everyone, "What would you change if you
  were me?"

- Listen, review, think.

Step two for the transformative CEO promoted
from within is to take a deep breath; psyche yourself to
get even more mentally and emotionally tough-minded;
and start making your three to eight "big change" to-do
list. That list might include retiring x number of coex-
ecutives, two of whom are neighbors. The insider CEO
knows the challenges, knows the weak players, knows

what must be done, but must act like an outside CEO who has no qualms about making changes.

Step three for both the outside and inside transformative CEO is to paint a picture of the new culture, the new way of doing things, the path to success, a crystal clear quantitative definition of performance, and how performance will be measured and compensated.

Step four is to start measuring.

5

Put Culture First and Forever

There are three sustaining factors in business: winning culture, marketing, and innovation. That's it. Three factors. Marketing is the identification, attraction, getting and keeping of okay customers. Innovation is creating new products, new ideas, new ways, new processes, new anything.

Having a profitable customer is the most important factor for company success. No customers; no company. No money; no mission. No pesos; no purpose. But it is the corporate culture that attracts, screens, and retains the kind of people who get and keep the company's target customers. It is the culture that lures the best, the brightest, the hungriest, the most innovative.

Good people may not fit in a good company's culture. That's okay. Not every good soldier wants to be a U.S. Marine. Not every top notch marketing person wants to work at Procter & Gamble. Not every buttoned-up MBA graduate can flourish in a buttoned-up company.

Company culture is an immune system: it works to protect the organization from intruders. A healthy immune system is crucial to any organization's existence.

Bernie Marcus (Founding CEO, Home Depot): "I had a boss who was the meanest S.O.B. who ever existed. He was proud of being mean and tough. He was a bully. He wanted people to fear him. He told me that when he fired someone, he wanted to hurt the person financially, emotionally, even physically. That loser taught me what a CEO should never be. I knew that I would build a company from scratch with values exactly opposite of my old boss.

"I wanted Home Depot to have a new kind of retailer culture, a transformative culture. I developed a culture based on marvelous customer service. I wanted every employee to know they worked *with*

Arthur Blank, my cofounder, and me, and *not for us*. We didn't just talk about being a true team, we proved it. Unlike other founders, owners, CEOs, Arthur and I did not take stock options. We owned enough stock to make us wealthy. We created 4,000 millionaires, many of them just high school graduates.

"And we were going to have a culture that helps the communities where our customers and employees live. Our communities know that if there is a problem where we can help, we will. Home Depot does not gouge customers looking to buy plywood before or after a devastating hurricane. We help board up our neighbors' windows. The winning, helping, sharing culture we built at our very beginning, in 1979, is alive and cherished today."

Tony Hsieh (CEO, Zappos): "Lots of companies have core values, but they usually end up as posters on the wall that nobody ever looks at. Zappos has ten core values and we make sure everyone in the company has those core values, and lives them."

Jim McCann (CEO, 1-800-Flowers): "It is tough to maintain your culture as you grow. Every time someone new comes into the company, or you add a new division, the culture is affected, influenced, even a little bit. My job is to be our 'cultural engineer.' So I am always thinking what things do we celebrate, what do we reward, and what do we simply not tolerate? And what kind of example am I setting? Should I set?"

In winning companies you can cut the culture with a knife. Every 16-year old knows that his motor vehicles department treats him differently than the local Starbucks does. There is a cultural difference between the people who work for the IRS and those who work for Doctors Without Borders.

A rich, strong culture is a competitive business strategy.

The Beekley Corp. innovates, makes and sells products that are used to improve diagnoses by radiologists. Beekley has the highest positives from customers than any of its competitors. But Beekley has a tough selling job. Competitors offer "almost as good" or "good enough" knock-off products at 30 to 80 percent lower prices than Beekley. Beekley's customers are in health care, an industry pummeled to reduce its prices, which, in turn, passes that pummeling on to its suppliers. Beekley sells its products via the phone. Beekley's "teleteachers" are motivated, well-trained, well-compensated, but selling over the phone can be painful.

These challenges are the rationale for one of the most unique, indeed incomparable, company cultures found anywhere.

Ayn LaPlant (CEO, Beekley Corp.): "Beekley created the business of diagnostic skin markers to help radiologists better read mammograms and x-rays. In the beginning our competition was makeshift markers. For example, an x-ray tech might tape a vitamin E pill on the patient. In the customer's eyes makeshift markers, a pill and tape, cost practically nothing. So from day one Beekley was both a missionary company, and a seller of value. Missionaries face rejection. We established a culture to reduce the pain of rejection, and to get high performance people."

Ayn LaPlant: "Our culture has many features. We have core values, and every single person in the company can quote these values from memory; and abides by them. We constantly focus on growth and innovation. Our new headquarters building is named the "Beekley

Growth and Innovation Center." Every day, every associate walks beneath that name. We are a learning culture. We have a psychology of achievement. We have a high-expectations, high-performance environment. Our associates invest up to 15 percent of their work time in training and learning programs, and these programs are aligned to someone's skill needs, experience, job function, and so on.

"We are big on symbols. For example, a core value is ARC: Attitude, Results, Continuous improvement. So we talk about 'getting aboard the ARC.' We offer 'lifeboats' to associates who are struggling. We 'make footprints,' that encourage associates to go where no one has gone before. We have lots of fun events. Celebrations. Bell ringing. Prizes. Raffles. 'High-stakes' bingo. Occasionally we will get a limo bus, the ARC, and winners will 'board the ARC' and continue to a celebration event."

Ayn LaPlant: "Our mission is to save lives by improving diagnoses. Our direct customers are medical facilities, and we totally believe in 'World Class Customer Care.' We are constantly talking and listening to our customers. World Class Customer Care, in part, means anticipating customers' needs and exceeding those needs. Instead of the traditional department designation such as marketing, manufacturing, finance, we have a 'Customer Care Team,' a 'Customer Enhancement Team,' a 'Customer Astonishment Team.'"

Culture is about the people and the way they interact with each other and with customers. Get the culture right, and you will always hire the right people, who will always do the right thing.

The transformative CEO is the custodian of the culture and the cultivator.

6

Hire to Your Culture

Every organization has a different vibe, a different rhythm, a different stroll. Companies are like tribes, with their own languages, spoken and unspoken, their own way of hunting and farming, their taboos, bloodlines, legacies. Survivor companies don't let you in, or let you stay, if you threaten their ways. Winning companies seek new members that will add strength, add vitality, add brains. Winning companies protect their cultures from disease, but they realize that time-dated thinking, unchallenged traditional thinking, uninspected conventional wisdom, are dangerous.

The CEO is the custodian of the organization's culture. The CEO ensures people are hired who will enliven the culture so it endures. The CEO makes it clear that regardless of talent or temperament, if somebody is negatively counterculture, that person leaves.

Sodexo Health Care cares about the patients and people it serves. Caring, improving quality of life, is Sodexo's purpose. Sodexo captured its purpose in the acronym CARES.

C is for compassion

A is for accountability

R is for respect

E is for enthusiasm

S is for service

Pat Connolly (President, Sodexo Health Care): "We care, we really care. We hire to CARES. Can the person meet our CARES requirements? We train to CARES. We compensate to CARES."

John Paul DeJoria (Founding CEO, Paul Mitchell Systems; Founder Patrón Spirits): "Our culture is about loving our people, loving our industry, and loving what we do. We only hire people with that attitude. If in three months, the newly hired person discovers he or she doesn't love the job, or we don't feel the love, then she or he leaves. We give him or her a great recommendation. It isn't her or his fault. We just weren't right for that person. You've got to love it. And many do. At John Paul Mitchell Systems, in over 30 years, our turnover has been less than 30 people."

Robert L. Johnson (Founding CEO, BET; Founder and Chairman, The RLJ Companies): "Our culture is based on ethics, value creation, and innovation. Culture is fundamental. People have to know how the culture functions, what is okay, good, and what is not done, or tolerated, in this company. If someone breaks with the culture, becomes a threat to our culture, he has to leave, even if he is the brightest of superstars. The CEO has to keep the culture alive and well. If the culture breaks down, if turf battles start, then innovation stops. That's the beginning of the end. Great companies have great cultures. You have to hire people who will buy into your culture and become true believers."

Tony Hsieh (CEO, Zappos): "Our culture is our number one priority as a company. We believe if we get the culture right, then our employees will do the right thing and create great experiences for our customers. We hire to our culture. We have one set of interviews to determine if the person has what we need. Then we do a separate set of interviews, purely for culture fit. She has to pass both to get hired. We make sure the person has the core cultural values we expect. For example, one of our values is to be humble. If someone is really egotistical, even if she is the greatest and most talented person, and we know she could do a lot for our top or bottom line, we won't hire her because she is not a culture fit."

Maxine Clark (Founder, CEO, Build-A-Bear Workshop): "We have two groups of employees, full-time and part-time. We hire and train to match our brand image, our culture. Consequently, among our full-time employees, we retain over 90 percent. Our retention rate among part-timers is twice the national average. What is interesting is that we hire teenagers and grandparents, who work next to each other. These two demographics fit our brand image. We hire people who care. We train on how to treat the customer. And then we let them care about the customer."

Shelly Lazarus (Chairman, Ogilvy & Mather): "We have a set of values, a set of principles, rules on how we treat each other. And everyone in O&M knows our mission. Our mission is to create advertising that builds brands, because good brands drive clients' sales. Our brand is known for building brands. Like our famous founder, David Ogilvy, demanded, we are focused on our clients, and on our clients' customers. David constantly reminded everyone that without clients we would not be in business. We respect our clients. We respect each other. We have nice people. We are a nice company. David used to say that, 'Ogilvy & Mather is a company of ladies and gentlemen with brains.' We have great respect for our clients' customer, the consumer. David had a famous line, 'The consumer is not a moron; she is your wife.' Of course, we have updated this view, adding, 'or he is your husband,' 'or your partner,' 'or your significant other.' Everyone at O&M loves our clients' customers. These principles say a lot about the kind of company we are, and about the kind of people we hire, and the kind of people who thrive here."

Hire to your culture. Your culture is your company's immune system. Hiring to your culture reduces the chance of infection.

7

Performing While Transforming

It is harder to transform a successful company than it is to fix a sick company. In a sick company everybody knows there are problems. Everybody knows something has to change, be it good or bad. In a successful company people are enjoying the vegetables of their labors. People don't want the good times to end, and they don't want to hear that things have to change.

The biggest problem in business is that the environment, the market, technology, and competitors change, but companies do not. Managements that are not always surveying their business environment will miss the sucker punch. Managements that see the barbaric hoards galloping to their door, and go ostrichical, or dance until dawn, should be arrested for management malpractice.

When the environment starts to change, and that change endangers the successful business model, the transformative CEO acts. He or she gathers the team, explains the need to rethink, gets everyone acting off the same playbook, and fires the starter gun.

Scott Davis became CEO of UPS at the beginning of a global recession. There was an unpredicted, and unprecedented, residential housing collapse; financial chaos in the banking sector, European currency and debt crises. The economic slowdown impacted markets around the world, and around the world is where UPS goes.

> **Scott Davis:** "Transformation is a strategic imperative. It is the CEO's job to manage the transformation. To speed it up if necessary. It means overcoming any resistance to change in the organization. It means disrupting the status quo. The CEO has to communicate his vision, and to keep everybody on board."

> **Scott Davis:** "I am fortunate that UPS has always been a visionary company, always looking into the future, and because we are over 100 years old, we've done transformational challenges before. In fact, our strategy embraces transformation. Our strategy is simple and straightforward: 'Create value, transform, and invest to grow.' During the global recession, and during

the slow economic recovery, we, and by 'we', I mean the 400,000-plus UPSers around the world, we crafted and implemented the following transformation plan:

- The surge in online shopping meant we had to better segment and redefine our customers. Online shipping dramatically increased the need to provide error-free, fast, friendly shipments to residences as opposed to businesses. We invested heavily to create and launch the innovative UPS My Choice, which gives consumers electronic control over the timing of their home deliveries. Over 500,000 consumers enrolled in three weeks.

- We made tough expense cutting decisions. We streamlined some businesses, but never cut into our core competency of providing superior logistics solutions.

- We continued to invest over $1 billion a year in technology, in telematics, analytics, package flow technology. Anything that helps our customers.

- We consolidated our small package operations, and pushed profit and loss responsibility, and marketing and sales resources, into local offices, where the UPSers are closer to the customer.

- We ramped up our investments to serve the special storage, package handling, and regulatory compliance requirements of the worldwide healthcare industry.

- To better serve our customers, who are also fighting through the recession, we increased our investment in Worldport, our global air hub. We opened a new intra-Asia air hub in Shenzhen."

Scott Davis: "We built a stronger company during difficult and uncertain times. UPS is well-positioned for whatever lies ahead."

Perform. Transform.

(Note: The authors were introduced to the concept of "performing while transforming" by Ron Frank, Managing Partner, Internal Consulting Practice, IBM Global Services. The concept came from an original IBM white paper, entitled, "Delivering Performance Through Continuous Transformation" written by Jim Dolan, Jim Bramante and Ron Frank in Sept., 2009.)

8

Have a Higher Purpose

The French have a wonderful phrase, "raison d'être." It means "reason to be." Reason to be, purpose, mission. Many grand companies have been established to achieve a higher purpose than simply making money. When successful, money often follows. Big money. Every good product, every good company fills a customer's need. There is nothing wrong with any ethical company that fills any need. That some companies, and their transformative leaders, choose to fill unpopular needs, or apparently unprofitable needs, or socially neglected needs, is good citizenship, good for their customers and stakeholders, and good for capitalism.

Arkadi Kuhlmann was dismayed at the way the American consumer was abandoning the habits of thrift and saving money, and instead was spending, and spending recklessly. He looked at the 9,600 banks in America. Their relentless marketing of credit, loans and credit cards was to Arkadi Kuhlmann, misleading the consumer, and dangerous.

> **Arkadi Kuhlmann (CEO, ING DIRECT):** "Credit cards are the opium of consumerism. The core of my idea was to bring Americans back to saving their money rather than spending it. There is a bank, two banks, four banks on every corner. That is a lot of money invested in rent, property taxes, people. I thought, let's help Americans save more by giving some of their money back to them. By putting a savings bank online we could return some or most of the costs of branch banks to our customers. No branches means no real estate, no tellers, no parking lots, and we're open 24 hours. I truly believe we have a higher purpose than banking. We are saving America, as we get Americans to save."

Despite onerous banking regulations, Arkadi Kuhlmann started ING DIRECT, and in ten years it became the largest savings bank in America with over $90 billion in assets.

Lynn Tilton is CEO of the largest female-owned business in America. Her company was founded for the purpose of saving American manufacturing. Her company, Patriarch Partners, has invested in over 150 U.S. manufacturing companies, almost all in serious trouble. Lynn Tilton says her company uses a "confluence of cash and creativity to turn around and rebuild distressed businesses."

> **Lynn Tilton:** "America was built on the thesis of people standing shoulder-to-shoulder to build industries, to build companies that create value through the production of goods and services. Somewhere along the line America lost its way as it forgot this founding principle. We can put idle assets and idle people back to work through the power of innovation. Our nation still lays claim to the greatest asset known to the world— our human capital."

> **Lynn Tilton:** "My purpose is to recreate a value-added America."

At last count Lynn Tilton's resurrection efforts have saved 250,000 American jobs.

> **Tony Hsieh (CEO, Zappos):** "The number one goal shouldn't be about money. It should be about making life better, and something you are passionate about. I say, 'chase the vision, not the money', and here at Zappos our vision is to bring a bit of happiness to the American consumer. And we bring happiness by delivering happiness. We deliver happiness to our customers, our employees, our owners, our vendors. Happiness is a pretty good purpose for a business."

John Paul DeJoria was raised by a single mom in a tough downtown Los Angeles neighborhood. John Paul's mom was a hard worker. John Paul and his brother got up at 5 a.m., folded the morning newspapers, and started delivering in the dark. John Paul and his brother pooled their money with what their mom made. One weekend, their combined financial resources amounted to 27 cents. John Paul's mother said, "boys we have food in the fridge. We have a little garden out back. We're happy. We aren't sick. We're rich!" John Paul DeJoria, cofounder of Paul Mitchell Systems, had 27 cents, but now the 27 is followed by zeros, lots of zeros.

> **John Paul DeJoria:** "Paul and I started Paul Mitchell Systems with $700. Our first rule was that we would

never test our products on animals. We would test the products on ourselves. That tells you something about our philosophies. I grew up in the inner city. I thought 'We have to help inner city youth.' Paul agreed. We had little money but in downtown L.A. we had some bad gangs: Crips, Bloods, Hispanic gangs, and other ethnic-based gangs. Everybody was fighting. So somehow we established a safe-haven house in L.A. It became a zone of neutrality among the gangs. Kids from grade school, junior high, and high school had a safe place to go. To be tutored. To live a little bit longer. We believed in the beginning that our business could make money and help people at the same time. We have other safe houses in the United States, and orphanages and homes for the elderly in Mexico, and other projects around the globe.

Our staff, and all our customers know that we can change societies, that we are changing societies, that we are definitely making good changes. And that makes us happy."

Robert Johnson became a billionaire with his innovative Black Entertainment Television. As BET became successful, Robert Johnson used the enterprise to create opportunities for minorities. He is now chairman of The RLJ Companies, a portfolio of over 15 companies, intentionally focused to improve educational opportunities for minorities, and to give people access to business acumen and financial resources.

Seth Goldman (CEO, Honest Tea): "I realized that tea is produced by some of the poorest countries in the world, but enjoyed by the wealthiest. There is a great opportunity to create wealth at a community level. When we are buying 25 million pounds of organic ingredients, we are going to make an impact on the environment: fewer pesticides and herbicides, and a better life for farmers.

"And from a health perspective, giving Americans a drink with a lot less sugar would be good for the American diet and help with the obesity crisis."

David Steiner (CEO, Waste Management): "I have three sons. I want to pass this planet on to them in better shape than I inherited it. This is a business where we can build shareholder value, make a lot of money, and materially improve our Earth. Our strategy of extracting value from waste is how we will save

the planet for my kids, and the kids of our wonderful
43,000 employees, and every other kid."

America is the most generous nation in the world.
America is the most innovative nation in the world. American corporations can do God's work. Having a higher
purpose is smart business.

9

Give Back

Transformative organizations are stunningly generous. Their people volunteer. The companies are philanthropic. They give back to their communities. They are serious about improving the environment. These superstar companies improve society by helping.

The culture of giving attracts special talent, is recognized by customers, and is daunting to competitors who just don't get it. Altruistic companies lead their industries in employee retention, employee morale, and employee pride. It is not a coincidence that generous companies have strong market share positions, are consistently profitable, have big brands, and are endlessly innovative.

Frances Hesselbein rose from Girl Scout to CEO, Girls Scouts USA. During her 14-year tenure as CEO she established the Daisy Scout program to attract young girls, increased minority membership, and added 2,250,000 new Girl Scouts.

> **Frances Hesselbein (CEO, Leader to Leader Institute):** "It's amazing what happens to the people in an organization when they are part of meeting a critical societal need. When you engage your own people, where do you find higher productivity, higher morale?"

Anne Mulcahy transformed Xerox from a stumbling, battered company back to greatness. After retiring as CEO, she became chairperson of Save the Children.

> **Anne Mulcahy (CEO, Xerox [ret.]; Chair, Save the Children):** "I believe that if you are privileged and fortunate enough to lead a commercial for-profit enterprise, and you have the opportunity to give back you should. Save the Children is doing just that. And I am having no problem getting support from generous corporations around the world."

In 2000, Pat McGovern and his wife, Lore Harp McGovern, pledged $350 million to establish The McGovern Institute for Brain Research at MIT. The McGovern Institute is led by a team of world-renowned neuroscientists committed to meeting two great challenges: understanding how the brain works and discovering new ways to prevent or treat brain disorders.

Pat McGovern (Founder and Chairman, International Data Group [IDG]): "This dream of understanding the human brain is now within our grasp, and we are convinced that its realization will be the greatest accomplishment of the twenty-first century. We are proud to play a part in making this happen."

Corporate philanthropy is a winning marketing strategy. Intelligent philanthropy is a smart use of shareholder money. Good corporate citizenship builds brands and begets customers.

Shelly Lazarus (Chairman, Olgivy & Mather): "The customers have spoken. Customers care whether or not companies are good citizens. A company's philanthropy signals what they are at their core. For example, the Ronald McDonald House is philanthropic and brand building. The Ronald McDonald House is a window into McDonald's core. Unilever owns Dove soap. Unilever put all its philanthropic dollars into a program to build self-esteem among girls aged 10 to 14. Unilever ran an ad on the Super Bowl that was not about Dove, per se, but about raising girls' self-esteem. That's smart brand building."

Dan Amos (CEO, Aflac): "Being a good corporate citizen means giving back to a cause you cherish. It's giving back to those who are in need because it is the right thing to do."

Philanthropy is literally in the DNA of General Mills. In 1866, a gentleman with the wonderful name of Cadwallader Washburn established General Mills by building one of the first flour mills in Minneapolis. General Mills had a devastating mill explosion in the 1880s. Mr. Washburn compensated every person who was adversely affected by the disaster, including establishing an orphanage that is still operating and active today.

Ken Powell (CEO, General Mills): "Our founder was an inspired benefactor, and such community caring has always been a hallmark of the General Mills culture. General Mills is one of the largest philanthropic givers in the country. More than 80 percent of General Mills U.S. employees volunteer in some way. We've got people in Africa helping solve food shortage problems. We have hundreds of scientists in our labs who want to help people. This is highly motivating for our employees. At General Mills, we refer to volunteerism as 'giving our employees the opportunity to live their values.'"

Philanthropy indeed builds brands and customer loyalty. The General Mills brand, Gold Medal Flour, has been the number one flour brand for 150 years. Wheaties was introduced in the 1920s, and is still a powerhouse brand. Cheerios is the best selling cereal brand in the United States.

Big brands and big philanthropy is not serendipitous.

John Paul DeJoria (Founding CEO, Paul Mitchell Systems and Founder Patrón Spirits): "It is simple: Success unshared is failure. Even the students in our

> hairdressing schools learn to give back. They hold fun-
> draisers which we call Cut-a-Thons. They raise money
> for charities, for their communities, their country, and
> the world. While they are in our schools, they learn to
> give back, and it makes them feel good. We help cre-
> ate vegetable gardens in the Appalachian Mountains.
> We feed thousands of orphans in Africa every single
> day. Success unshared is failure.

Jim Gillespie was a brand new real estate agent starting out, and had no money. He represented a poor, elderly couple in selling their house. He sold the house,
his second sale, and gave back his entire commission to
his clients. Years later, Jim Gillespie is CEO, Coldwell
Banker, leading 87,000 global agents and employees.

Jim Gillespie has given back in another exceptional
way. Of the five chief operating officers (COOs) who
worked for Jim Gillespie, four have become CEOs of
other leading residential and commercial real estate
companies.

> **Jim Gillespie:** "I don't believe real estate profession-
> als, or anyone else should work for nothing. But, if you
> are in your job just for the money, you may forget that

your purpose is to help people. Those who help the most, often benefit the most financially. Giving the commission back was the right thing at the time. I never did it again."

Jim Gillespie: "For the record, I am proud that four of my COOs have gone on to be CEOs in their own right. I always try to hire good people who have big talent and will mesh within our culture. I guess other organizations also like who we hire and why."

Panasonic is positively impacting society in a unique and dramatic way. Panasonic has made a global commitment to becoming a leader in environmental innovation. Joe Taylor, CEO, Panasonic, is moving the North American headquarters from a 50-acre suburban corporate campus in Secaucus, New Jersey, to a state-of-the-art, environmentally sound office tower the company is building in downtown Newark, NJ.

Joe Taylor: "We are moving to a site adjacent to Newark's Penn Station, which is an incredible public transit hub. We will keep 1,000 jobs in New Jersey; help transform what was once a great city; save money; and take advantage of a teachable moment for our employees. We are telling our people that we can't have 1,000 employees individually commuting back and forth in 1,000 cars every day, and be a legitimate environmental improvement leader. Moving to Newark will reduce the collective Panasonic gas consumption, reduce carbon emissions, reduce road congestion, and so on, in a major way. The lesson is that doing something good for our planet is a personal and corporate responsibility, and not something to delegate to activists. And our employees will save money, the publicity will touch our customers, and Newark gets a fabulous corporate citizen."

Give and get. Give money; get customers.
Give time; get positive brand awareness.
Transform communities; transform society.

10

Nothing Is Impossible

Unless you know the future of science, of technology, of the affairs of man, then you can count on one historical reality: things will change, and what yesterday was impossible, today is a female voice in your car telling you to turn right in a mile. Transforming an obstinate, negative culture is hard, but not impossible. Turning around a behemoth company, or a company in a coma, is not impossible. Launching products that fly to the moon, that can see through concrete, that can think, are not impossible . . . anymore.

What is impossible is an answer, a solution, not yet imagined.

Challenge the organization. Push the organization. Keep the pressure on for creativity, innovation, differentiation. Be relentless in getting change and performance.

Every day a company pops up somewhere offering the world a product that yesterday was considered to be impossible.

Daniel Lamarre (CEO, Cirque du Soleil): "Every day at Cirque starts with one question: 'What is there that's impossible that I can try to achieve today?' That's every day. It's easy to repeat the same thing, to get comfortable, to use the same formula. If we don't challenge ourselves we might stop innovating."

Royal Caribbean Cruises transformed its industry by doing what one could never imagine being done at sea. A customer while aboard the biggest passenger ships in the world can choose to ice skate on the equator. Or sunbathe while cruising past glaciers. Or go rock climbing at sea. Or ride a full-size carousel. The physically adventurous can ocean surf on the Flow Rider, a surfing simulator, which is CEO Richard Fain's favorite activity while on the ship.

Richard Fain: "Our advertising describes us as the 'Nation of Why Not.' And that is absolutely true. We really do believe in 'Why not.' We asked ourselves, can we build the grandest ships on the sea, where the internal center of the ship can be opened to the sky? Our answer: 'Why not?' And so we did. We continue to do the unexpected. All of us at Royal Caribbean believe that anything is possible. Our customers love our innovative surprises."

Bill Roedy (Founding CEO, MTV International): "There were significant challenges in establishing MTV in the global marketplace. Distribution was a huge problem. There was not an infrastructure to carry MTV. Getting advertisers to bet on an unproved concept, to take a risk, was another difficulty. And regulations everywhere. Ownership regulations. Airwave regulations. Border regulations. The French regulations are legendary. But if you don't take no for an answer, and if you have the proper attitude of 'respect and reflect' for the local culture and people, you can overcome any challenge."

Do the impossible before a competitor or an upstart, who has the imagination, and the gumption, disproves prevailing wisdom.

"They said it couldn't be done," is a high compliment for the transformative CEO.

11

Take the Risk

Risk is at the heart of transforming a company. Starting a new industry, launching a new product, reinventing a company, turning a draft horse into a racehorse require risk taking. Changing strategy is a risk. Investing in nascent technology is a risk. Not investing in opportunity is a risk. Ironically, it is risk-averse managements that create the need for transformative CEOs. Risk-averse managements pull back in tough times; shrink from change in tough times; cut investments that get and keep customers.

How does the transformative CEO think about risk?

Mark Dixon (Founder; CEO, Regus): "Being a CEO is about leadership, making tough decisions, making mistakes. You have to be prepared to take risks. It's just leadership."

Bill Roedy (Founding CEO, MTV International): "As you develop a business, you have to take risks. This is an important principle. Break the rules. You're going to make mistakes, but that's how you learn."

Willy Walker (CEO, Walker & Dunlop Co.): "We are one of the most respected financiers of multifamily housing in the country, and have been in this industry for three generations. In 2008 we faced a meltdown in the housing market. Our capital sources include Fannie Mae and Freddie Mac, and they were blistered on the front pages every day. Interest rates were all over the place. Big banks, investment banks, big lenders, went out of business, or were stampeding to the exit door. So we thought things through. Evaluated all kinds of risks. Figured where we thought our world was heading. Then we doubled down, tripled down. On ourselves. On our expertise. We eliminated a dilutive co-company brand name. We acquired a company with exceptional people. We invested to bring on super talent at every level of the company. We opened offices across the country. We put together the finest, hardest charging team of producers, sales people, in our industry. And we went public. There was risk,

> but as the CEO transforming a family company, but a jewel of a company, into a NYSE traded company, I adhered to the athlete's maxim, 'You can't win if you aren't in the game'. And we are so in the game."

Dan Amos is CEO of Aflac, Inc., an insurance company. Insurance companies think about risk like bees think about pollen. Insurance companies' risk analyses include careful calculations and estimates of the probabilities of an adverse event occurring; adequate coverage and premiums; exposure to disaster payouts.

Dan Amos is an expert on risk management, and has built a company where everyone is trained to evaluate their decisions according to three principles:

First, don't risk a lot for a little.

Second, don't risk more than you can afford to lose.

Third, consider the odds, the probabilities of something, anything occurring.

Dan Amos wanted to build the Aflac brand name. He decided to do so by retooling Aflac's television commercials. He applied his three principles of risk management to the evaluation of a potential Aflac Duck creative advertising campaign.

> **Dan Amos:** "The commercial production and media campaign would cost $1 million, which is a lot of money, but if it worked, it would mean millions in revenue to Aflac. OK, passed the first principle.
>
> "As for not risking more than you can afford, we would not like to lose a million dollars, but we could afford it. If the commercial did not work, we would pull it off the air immediately, and cut our loss.
>
> "Finally, rule three, consider the odds. This was the tricky part. Our research told us the 'Duck' commercial tested 150 percent better than any commercial we had ever tested. Our previous best commercial tested a brand recognition score of average. I was sick of average.
>
> "We tested a traditional 'feel-good' commercial with Ray Romano and some kids playing with blocks that spelled Aflac. That concept tested 50 percent better than our prior best commercial. So my dilemma was whether to go with the feel-good, or go with a wildcard duck commercial that made fun of our brand name?

"I asked another CEO what he thought, and his exact words were, 'Nobody ever got fired for a 50 percent increase. Go with Ray Romano.' That was the safe bet.

"But the third principle is to consider the odds. The Duck scored higher. Better odds. So I went with the Duck.

"When I told people the new commercial would feature a duck that quacks 'Aflac,' the response was always the same: a silent stare. Fortunately, the Aflac Duck commercials have become one of the most memorable and successful ad campaigns ever. I think back and realize I risked my entire career on that darn duck! Always consider that odds really paid off."

The difference between the corporate executive and the entrepreneur is that the corporate guy can hear "yes" 99 times and "no" once, and will abort. The entrepreneur can hear "no" 99 times and "yes" once, and plunge ahead.

The transformative CEO understands these mind-sets, and leads, and goes with the Duck.

12

Obstacles Are Opportunities

The transformative CEO, by definition, faces obstacles. The company is on life support or the market is tanking or there is no money or a new technology is making the workhouse product obsolete. Obstacles are legion, constant, daily, and deadly. The transformative CEO analyzes the obstacle. He or she does not shrink, or wring hands. The transformative CEO asks of himself, and all others, "How can we take advantage of this challenge? What can we do that no one else would even attempt? How do we win?"

Ralph de la Vega, CEO, AT&T Mobility, and his family were planning to leave Cuba for America. At the last minute, Fidel Castro's government decreed: "Only the boy can go." Ralph de la Vega was 10 years old. He left Cuba alone, and arrived in a land where he did not speak the language, could not read the signs, did not like the food. He stayed with a wonderful family in Miami, who treated him like a son for four years, until his parents finally made it to Florida.

> **Ralph de la Vega:** "Looking back at that event, I would not change a thing. It turned my life for the better. Now I always look for the opportunity in obstacles, and that outlook is a hallmark of my career."

> **Ralph de la Vega:** "Just as I took over the wireless business in Latin America the bottom fell out. Argentina went into an absolute depression. Not a recession; a full depression. The currency was devalued by 75 percent. Our company's Argentine revenues fell overnight from $1 billion a year to $250 million. Our business plan was short $750 million. Then the problem worsened. We had to buy phones in dollars, but got paid in pesos. So our selling price quadrupled."

The challenge was to maintain some profitability despite losing $750 million in revenues, and to lead a salesforce whose product was totally priced out of the market.

The de la Vega Obstacle/Opportunity Action Plan

- Stop selling.

- Turn salespeople into bill collectors.

- Collect every unpaid peso.

- Slash costs.

- Reorganize, restructure every piece of the business to lower the breakeven.

Result: revenues down; margins up; customers saved; salesforce preserved; company saved.

> **Ralph de la Vega:** "The bottom line in transforming a company is to have a good vision, a well-executed plan, and people who are passionate and engaged. Then people can surmount incredible challenges."

John Paul DeJoria was waiting for funds from an investor who was putting in the money to fund their start-up. It was 1980, a terrible economic time. Interest rates were 18 to 20 percent. Unemployment was 10.5 percent. Iran held U.S. hostages. People waited for hours in line to get gasoline. The investor backed out. John Paul DeJoria had a few hundred dollars in his pocket.

He was also homeless and a single dad taking care of his 2½-year-old son.

John Paul DeJoria: "The times were tough. But we started the company anyway. There were lots of obstacles, but we saw a big opportunity in selling innovative products directly to hairdressers, who would use them on their customers, and then sell the products to their customers. We were going to give our hair salon owners products not available in retail stores. The salon owners would not have to compete with retailers. They were professionals and could give customers their professional recommendations. We came up with a single application shampoo that saved the stylists time and money. We came up with a hair conditioner that was also a cutting lotion, which made cutting and blow-drying faster and better. We had lots of other cool product ideas. Our goal was to, one day, do $5 million a year. Little did we know we would sell hundreds of millions."

John Paul DeJoria: "My way of handling obstacles is simple: I keep going. Entrepreneurs should be prepared for a lot of rejection. People say no in a million ways. If you knock on 100 doors and they all say no, then at door 101, be just as enthusiastic as you were at door number one. The opportunity is door 101. The big difference between successful people and unsuccessful people is that successful people do what no one else wants to do. Everyone intellectually knows you have to knock on door 101, or 201, and be up and positive. But only a few do it. Believe in yourself. Believe what you are selling is the best. Make sure your product or service is good quality. Then knock on as many doors as you have to."

Seth Goldman (CEO, Honest Tea Company): "When I started Honest Tea, I knew nothing about the beverage business. Good thing I didn't, as the unknown obstacles ultimately showed up. For example, distribution: how do we sell and distribute to thousands of stores? I made a call on some beverage distributors who turned us down. Big obstacle. You can't sell a product, even an innovative product, like Honest Tea if it is not on the shelves. So we found a cheese distributor. He sold Honest Tea to gourmet shops. We found a corned beef distributor who sold to delis.

We found a charcoal distributor who was going to grocery stores. We got into as many stores any way we
could. These nontraditional beverage distributors established our brand."

Aflac saw its brand awareness jump from 11 percent
to 93 percent due to its imaginative Aflac Duck television
commercials. In addition to the highly recognizable Duck,
the Duck's voice was also memorable. Then, in 2011, in
the midst of coping with an earthquake and tsunami in
Japan, home to 75 percent of Aflac's business, the person
who was the voice of the company's beloved Duck dis-
paraged and made fun of the tragedy. This insult put all
of the Duck's positive brand awareness in great jeopardy.

Dan Amos (CEO, Aflac): "We were sickened when we
heard of the incident. It was hard to believe that we had
to deal with it at a time when thousands of customers were dead or missing. Without hesitation, I fired
the actor. We created a silent movie style commercial so that we could maintain our brand awareness
while we started a nationwide search for someone to
be the new Aflac Duck. What at first seemed to be

an unbelievable challenge, turned out to be a public relations bonanza. 12,371 people auditioned for the job, and more than 70,000 media stories were generated about the search for a new voice. We turned a huge obstacle into a GIANT opportunity. I received a note from someone in the television business who, for over 20 years, has coordinated news for affiliate stations all over the country. The note read: 'Your reaction to the negative voice incident is the best example of turning a black eye into a beauty mark that I have seen in the public relations world . . . perhaps ever.'"

Public failure—in the press, on television, in the laughing competitors' boardrooms, amidst friends—is not a happy time. Nor is losing 75 percent of company revenues a happy time. Nor is being a young child alone, watching your mom, dad, and homeland disappear behind you. Nor is being homeless. Nor is facing the loss of the most famous Duck on the planet.

Business life can be tough. Mistakes are made. Bad luck happens. Banks call loans. Customers go away. Competitors serve devastating surprises. Colleagues disappoint. New products fail. Stockholders rail.

Leadership is needed when the creditors are calling; the predators are howling; and when the music isn't playing.

Leadership is finding opportunities regardless of the obstacle, the challenge.

To transformative CEOs, the *O* in *obstacle* is the start of *opportunity*.

13

Expensive Customer Service Is Free

Zappos is the phenomenal company that created a virtual shoe store. The Zappos customer never has to visit a shoe store. She never has to worry if the store in the mall has the perfect pair of shoes. She does not need to drive, park, wait for service, waste time. She never has to worry if the shoes will fit, or if the color will match her new outfit. She can order on any day, at any time, and get her shoes in one or two days. She never has to worry about returning shoes for any reason: just send them back . . . for free! And she can wait one year to return the shoes . . . for free! If she has any question, she can call any time, at 3 a.m. or 3 p.m. on Thanksgiving, and immediately get an answer, or have the problem solved. She never has to pay for anything, other than the shoes.

If you are a Zappos customer, and it's Wednesday, and you need one pair of shoes for Saturday, but you are not sure about the shoe size, or its color, or its comfort, simply order 10 pairs of shoes. Zappos will immediately ship them for free. Pick the pair you want and send the other nine pairs back to Zappos, for free! Then put on those shoes and knock them out on Saturday night.

Zappos has one business building strategy: it provides unmatched, super costly, wicked fast customer service for a mass market. No other company spends as much money per order, per customer than Zappos. (There are other superb consumer market customer service providers such as the Ritz-Carlton and Virgin Airlines, but they cater to smaller, select market segments.)

Efficiency experts and cost cutters and sharp-penciled financial folks would hyperventilate reviewing Zappos' wasteful, counter-intuitive customer service strategy. Here is what Zappos does that no other company would even consider:

- Has live human beings available to speak to the customer on every order, every hour of the year.

- Customer service reps do not try to up sell, or cross sell the customer.

- Customer service reps will spend an hour on the phone even if there is no sale. No problem.

- If a desired pair of shoes is out-of-stock, Zappos directs customers to competitors.

- The warehouse is open every hour of the year. This means 8,700 hours when lights are on, phones are used, packages packed, three shifts are paid, trucks loaded, and a hundred other warehousing "no should dos." This is a hugely inefficient way to run a warehouse.

- For clothes, there is free overnight shipping to the customers, and free return shipping.

- The vast majority of customers get a surprise, free shipping upgrade for overnight delivery.

Tony Hsieh, (Zappos CEO), "Because we invest in customer service, we don't have to spend a lot of money on advertising and other marketing. Our customers do our marketing. We deliver happiness and our customers deliver their friends and relatives to Zappos.

"'Expensive customer service creates millions of salespeople who work for us for free.'"

14

How to Innovate

Managements know they must innovate. They know they must change, adapt, differentiate, take some risk. Yet some managements are so tethered to their past, to their silos to the way it was, that they can't, won't, or don't know how to innovate.

Here are some public secrets on how to innovate.

- *Innovation starts at the top.* If the leader talks innovation, gives lots of examples, rewards attempts, lionizes successes, the organization gets the message. There is more untapped innovation in most companies than there are mussels on the Santa Monica pier.

- *Innovation is an idea turned into reality.* Creative ideas that are sketches on a pad, or the subject of unanswered e-mails are nothing. To innovate you must execute. And poor execution is not a reason to execute (as in terminate) the innovator or the idea.

- *The innovative company is always trying to improve.* Leadership talks new products, new markets, new machines. The company budgets aggressively on research, engineering, customer contact, smart people, commercialization.

- *Match ingenious engineers, or development people, with genius marketing people.* This is the most important rule for new product success.

- *Listen to customers.*

- *Have a high tolerance for rule breakers, as it relates to innovation, but not for breaking the company's culture rules.*

- *If someone proposes a promising idea, assign the development of the idea to that person.*

Bill Roedy (Founding CEO, MTV International): "We had this highly successful franchise, with lots of popular shows, but the content was all designed for the American market. If you are only targeting Americans, that's fine. But if you are going to be global, you need to innovate your products to reflect and be relevant to local customers, especially with media. It's not one cola or one burger, but instead a TV channel that reflects and respects local cultures. The brand name is the same, but innovation is needed to adapt the product to meet the differing consumer tastes in Brazil or India or South Korea."

Differentiation is innovation. Your differentiation, your product or service point-of-difference, need not be "better" than a competitor's, just different. The folks in your local breakfast spot who smile, are different than the bored, indifferent waitress down the street. You must differentiate your product, particularly if your competition is big and dominant.

Griffin Hospital is a small 160-bed community hospital. In each direction of the compass, just 12, or so, miles away, there is a major hospital. The people in the Griffin Hospital's market area can drive 12 miles and get care at large city hospitals including the well-known Yale-New Haven.

Patrick Charmel (CEO, Griffin Health Services): "At the outset of my career, I knew intuitively what I now know empirically; talk to the consumer. The consumer is the inspiration for innovation. If you probe, and if you listen, the consumer will tell you what she likes, dislikes, her concerns. The consumer usually won't give you the answers. Getting the answer is the job of the problem solver, not the problem sufferer.

"Our first big differentiation at a time when our survival was dependent on our ability to differentiate our hospital from the six competing hospitals that surrounded us was inspired by talking to expectant mothers. They indicated that they did not want giving birth to be treated like a medical emergency or illness care event. Mothers did not want to be exposed to sick patients or the traditional hospital environment. They did not want the visitation rules that were standard protocol in hospitals. We changed everything. We built a special entrance just for the mother and her family. We changed the maternity ward to look more like a home than a hospital. This was a radical change from how traditional maternity care was delivered. Gone was the restrictive one-size-fits-all approach. It was replaced by a personalized approach based on patient empowerment and family involvement. Changes to the care environment included the creation of large private postpartum rooms with beautiful finishes and furniture, some with the country's first queen-size hospital beds and Jacuzzis for pain relief in early labor. We made many other such consumer-centric changes. Most of our older, male, 'that's not the way it's done' doctors left. We replaced them with younger, more enlightened obstetricians. Our maternity business boomed, and we took what we learned to develop a patient-centered care model for the rest of the hospital.

"To complete our transformation, Griffin collaborated with the Planetree organization, a not-for-profit founded by a patient dissatisfied with her hospital experience, to change the way hospitals and doctors interact with and care for patients. Griffin ultimately acquired the Planetree organization and has grown its membership organization and consultancy by helping hospitals transform their cultures to deliver true patient-centered care. Health care providers are now dealing with educated, engaged, informed consumers. Health care organizations that understand and respond to changing consumer expectations will be their industry's new leaders. This understanding will be a game changer in health care."

Mark Dixon (CEO, Regus): "A big part of innovation is keeping your eyes open as you travel around the world, watching for new ideas, no matter where they may occur. Deliberately search for new and interesting ideas. As part of that search, talk and listen to everyone. If an idea is worth pursuing, start testing concepts, and test and review and adapt fast. Very fast. Review test results daily. Speed. Immediacy. Immediate execution of trials. Immediate results. Immediate adaptation. Once you're ready to go, get the right people. And execute, execute, execute."

Maxine Clark (Founder and CEO, Build-A-Bear Workshop): "When a 10-year old girl innocently asked, 'Why can't we make our own teddy bears?', the lightbulb flashed. My dream for Build-A-Bear Workshop was born. Every adult I asked about the idea said it would not work. But every kid asked, 'When can I build my bear?' Innovation is being different. And being different is the reason for our success. We didn't invent the teddy bear: we invented how to personalize and sell more teddy bears and other furry friends business. We followed our dream and did so with true passion. Now we have over 400 stores worldwide, and 100 million furry friends adventuring around the globe. We are beary happy."

Innovation is a sustaining factor in business. If a company fails to innovate, you can be certain a competitor will jump ahead, will change the way the old game was played. Somebody, somewhere, in a garage, or in a lab, or in a classroom, or homeless in a car, is working imaginatively, feverishly to make obsolete your product, your advantage. This somebody is unencumbered by your years of doing it your way; is not burdened with your investments in yesteryear equipment; is not concerned about failure.

Innovate or stagnate.

Differentiate or disintegrate.

Take your pick.

Make Everything Better, Better, Better!
(Including What Is Already "Perfect")

The egg has been a symbol of perfection for millennia. Medieval alchemists saw the egg as a symbol of perfection, as did most early civilized societies. The egg's seamless form makes it a common metaphor for perfection throughout poetry, literature, and art. The architecture of the egg is the circle, also a symbol of perfection. The shape of the egg, any egg, its ovality, its infinite circularity is considered nature's most elegantly simple design. The egg, the source of life, is perfect.

Egg sellers imply they have the perfect product. Egg sellers relentlessly remind consumers to buy the "incredible edible egg." But generic egg sales are plummeting.

Ordinary egg sales have fallen by 2 billion eggs per year. The perfect product isn't so perfect in the supermarkets ... except for the truly incredible Eggland's Best egg.

Eggland's Best (EB) has had double-digit growth for 179 of 180 consecutive months. EB has grown every month for 15 years, and sales growth is ever increasing.

What is the secret, the black box, and the magic behind EB's amazing counter-trend success? Simple, like the egg, EB improved the egg. EB now sells a better egg. Eggland's Best improved on perfection.

The cholesterol scare of the late early 1980s caused people to stop, or cut back on eating eggs. Egg consumption went from 365 eggs per person a year to 234 eggs per person per year. Consumers still wanted eggs, but they wanted healthy eggs. This led to the invention of Eggland's Best eggs in the early 1990s. Charlie Lanktree, CEO of Eggland's Best, gathered his small team and asked, "What if we made a better egg? What if we improved on Mother Nature?" (Note: Charlie Lanktree did not ask, "Can we make a better egg?" Or, "Why can't we make a better egg?" Those questions imply limits).

It was a "Eureka" moment. It was a text messenger's "OMG" moment. A better egg went on the market. EB's eggs are proven to have better taste and better nutrition than ordinary eggs. They have statistically less cholesterol, 25 percent less saturated fat, 300 percent more Omega 3, 200 percent more vitamin D than ordinary eggs, 10 times more vitamin E, 38 percent more lutein for vision, plus more vitamins B_{12} and B_5.

When the EB team transformed the making of the egg, they transformed the egg industry. Egg consumption is growing because EB sells more than 3 million eggs a year. EB totally changed the chicken's diet. They eliminated such cheap feed as animal fat, animal by-products, and reprocessed food. They implemented a high-cost, all-natural, all-vegetarian diet including EB-harvested sea kelp from the frigid waters of the North Sea.

> **Charlie Lanktree:** "We are feeding our chickens a very expensive diet. And our chickens can't cheat on their diets! After we made a better egg, we decided to make everything else at EB better."

> **Charlie Lanktree:** "We bettered the profits for EB, our farmers, and our retailers. We charge more for our better egg. Thus making more money for everyone. We bettered the industry's test standards. The total egg industry does about 200–300 quality and inspection tests per year. EB does 45,000 tests per year!

The USDA inspects all egg processing plants according to EB standards, which are unsurpassed. We are currently working to better our advertising, our packaging, our branding, our IT systems, our store distribution, and our people. We just introduced 'Hard Cooked Peeled Eggs' you can buy in your grocery store. Do a blind taste test and compare our convenient 'Hard Cooked Peeled Egg' with any other. Decide for yourself which egg tastes better. Our better eggs are The Best. Eggland's Best."

Thomas Edison is credited with 1,093 U.S. patents, including the lightbulb. No other person holds more patents than Edison. Although a prodigious inventor, Edison only worked on what already existed (for example, he did not invent the lightbulb. It had been in existence for 50 years prior to Edison's patent). According to Edison, "I try to make things better."

Heed Mr. Edison and Eggland's Best: make everything better.

16

Defend Ideas

You have heard it a thousand times in one clichéd form or another: "That won't work." Three little words. "That won't work." Three little words more deadly to innovation, growth, and transformation than the Ebola virus. If "that won't work" is part of the company culture, if it is the secret language of the saboteurs of change, then the transformative CEO must get out the scalpel.

Because marketing, innovation, and a winning culture are the only three sustaining factors in a business, then anything that imperils innovation must be eliminated. Eliminate those whose response, spoken or in deeds, is always a variation of "that won't work." Eliminate risk-averse people, risk-averse budgeting, risk-averse policies, and get rid of compensation plans that reward the risk averse.

Shelly Lazarus, chairman of Ogilvy & Mather, works in an idea industry, and in a brand building and advertising company that is an idea factory. Her job is to inspire ideas, defend ideas, and bring ideas to fruition.

> **Shelly Lazarus:** "O&M is a wonderful company. Every day there are new ideas. There is nothing as exciting as when I get a call from one of our people who says, 'I had an idea over the weekend. Can I stop by and tell you?' I can't wait to hear the idea, yet at the same time I know it's endangered. From a practical standpoint, ideas are really fragile. It is so easy to kill an idea, especially in the early stages. So I am an idea defender. Someone has to stand up and say, 'This idea is fantastic. Let's do it.' That's my job."

Charlie Lanktree, CEO of Eggland's Best, wanted to reinforce his brand name by putting their "EB" logo, in blue, or red, on every egg they sold.

> **Charlie Lanktree:** "I heard 'that's impossible.' 'It can't be done.' 'Eggshells are too fragile to get stamped

with the iconic EB.' And so on. Impossible is not the EB way. Now 3 billion times a year, every time one of our customers touches our egg, she sees 'EB'. How's that for building brand awareness?"

Defend ideas. Defend idea people. Praise attempts. Praise successes. Forget about the losers, but only if the losing idea received some objective review.

There is one certainty: If you, or your organization, believe it won't work, and you don't try, then you will be correct.

17

Lead with Love

That's right. Lead with love. Not romantic love, of course. Maybe tough love. Or quiet love. Parental love. Some kind of love. Love what you do. Love your company. Love your customers. It's infectious. What you love, your colleagues will love. Love making the sale. Love innovation. Love to go to work every day.

> **John Paul DeJoria:** "The culture of our organization is to love ourselves, love our families, love the people around us, and spread love and goodwill and good works throughout the world. By loving yourself you are going to be a happy person. Customers and colleagues prefer to work with happy people. 'If you are involved with Patrón Spirits or Paul Mitchell Salon hair care products, you've got to love the product, you've

got to love your customer, and you've got to love our planet Earth."

Kip Tindell (Founder; CEO, Container Store): "We have this yummy, employee-first culture that we all love. People join our company and never leave."

Pat Connolly (President, Sodexo Health Care): "I've never had a bad day at work."

Kathy Cloninger (former CEO, Girl Scouts of the USA): "It's all about the girls. And to be a sister to every Girl Scout."

Dan Warmenhoven (Executive Chairman, NetApp): "We have over 11,000 employees and they love the environment. They love that their recommendations are heard and they then get to implement their ideas. This is a great place to work. The people love what they do. They love whom they work with, and they love whom they work for. We do objective, blind surveys of our customers, and I must say, after reviewing the feedback, 'to know us is to love us.' That's the style of the organization we are trying to build."

There it is. Lead with love. If Stephen Stills would permit a slight change to his lyrics, "Love the ones you're with."

18

Leadership Is Not a Friendship Contest

Transforming a moribund company, transforming a dysfunctional culture, creating a new industry, turning around a company is not for the needy personality, constantly requiring approval and "atta boys." The transformative CEO is tough-minded. He or she must make tough decisions. And right or wrong, tough decisions impact, disrupt, interrupt, redirect, and shake up the organization. There will be people, maybe lots of people, who will be unhappy.

Changing the compensation system to pay for performance will make the mediocre unhappy. Retiring the popular, but change-resistant executive, will be unpopular with his locked-in-the-past fellow travelers. Encouraging prudent risk taking, praising the innovative, impatience with the stodgy and laggard, upsets the status quo. Bringing in outside talent, each with a keen understanding of the new way, will irritate those passed over or those moved over.

Peter Cuneo turned around six other consumer product businesses in addition to Marvel Entertainment. "For me, the human principle crucial to success, particularly when you must transform an enterprise, is the realization that a leader cannot make everyone happy. An effective leader never fears the critics and naysayers. He or she implements the changes that will propel an organization forward, without worrying about his or her popularity."

Doug Conant turned around Campbell Soup. "Over three years I systematically reviewed performance and made the tough calls. We replaced 300 of 350 managers."

Admiral John Paul Jones (1747–1792) believed that friendship was antithetical to leadership. Jones counseled his officers to be "fair, firm, and friendly . . . but not a friend." This management principle is still a fundamental tenet in the U.S. Navy's leadership training. John Paul

Jones is famous for his retort to a taunting British naval officer. "I have not yet begun to fight."

George Steinbrenner restored the New York Yankees to its historic winning ways. During the period of rebuilding, "The Boss" fired Billy Martin and Yogi Berra, two of the most popular Yankees of all time. According to George Steinbrenner, "I love those guys, but I love the Yankees more. What I did, I did for the organization. I hear the boos, and I read the newspapers, but I don't care. Sportswriters aren't going to help us win the World Series."

Transformative leaders must institute changes needed to win, and eliminate people, products, processes, policies, that are in the way. Forget the opinion polls and do the right thing.

19

Be Aware of
Your Wake

Boats that don't leave a wake aren't moving. The transformative CEO is always moving, always creating a wake. The transformative CEO is moving against the flows, causing an impressive wake. In some way, his or her wake always impacts every person in the organization. The wake can be a little ripple, dramatic, misinterpreted, positive, negative, fear-causing.

Be aware of your wake. Be completely aware of what you say, what you write, what you do. Every single action causes waves that rock the organization to some degree. Communicate clearly and carefully.

Kip Tindell (CEO, Container Store): "Being aware of your wake means knowing that everything you do, and everything you don't do, impacts your business and those around you. It means taking great care in ensuring that your communication is consistent, thoughtful, and transparent. It means leading with love, not fear. Caring about the impact you have on the organization and all of its stakeholders—its employees, customers, suppliers, communities—instills trust and makes the company stronger and more sustainable."

There is no such thing as a "no wake zone" in a transforming organization.

20

On Decision Making

President George W. Bush said, "I am the decider." Politics and personality aside, he was right (despite the clumsy word choice). Bush was the leader. Leaders must make decisions, often on the most difficult challenges facing the organization.

Here are some suggestions to inform and improve your decision making:

- Groups are smarter than individuals. Get advice. Listen to everyone.

- Have a "Kitchen Cabinet" (first used by President Andrew Jackson in 1832). A kitchen cabinet is one or more honest advisors who are usually not part of the leader's organization.

These people never knowingly let the leader make a mistake.

- Determine exactly when the decision must be made. If the decision has to be made in 60 seconds, think for 59 seconds.

- There is always ambiguity, a lack of certainty, a lack of crucial data. Strong leaders deal better with ambiguity than weak leaders.

- Decision making starts with knowledge. There are countless sources of knowledge including your years of experience, observation, instincts, street savvy education.

- Advisors always come from a vantage point. Be sure you know what those vantage points are to better assess the advice.

- Facts come with interpretations. Be sure you know the difference, and know all the interpretations.

- Don't always believe what you think. Fight your natural tendency to embrace "motivated reasoning," "motivated belief," and "bias confirmation." Recognize that you may be subconsciously looking for facts and arguments that support your position. You may be rejecting facts that are contrary to your position. Fight hard to be objective. Motivated reasoning, rationalizing our beliefs, rationalizing our past decisions, almost always trumps facts.

- Zealots do not believe contradictory facts, scientific evidence, even what they witness with their own eyes.

- Always doubt: it opens the mind to new solutions. Assume nothing.

- Determine "What is the worst outcome that can happen?" Often the "worst that can happen" is manageable.

- Probabilities. Probabilities. Probabilities. Based on your experience, and that of your group, fashion some mathematical probability of something happening or not happening. The police park at the same spot on the highway three days a week. What is the probability that you will get a speeding ticket? What is the cost of that ticket?

- Reduce your confidence level in what you think you know by 50 percent. You are a leader. You are always overconfident. What does anyone really know for certain? Not much. Be modest in what you think you know.

- Figure out all the "unintended consequences." "Unintended consequences" is a cop-out excuse for politicians, not CEOs. Unintended consequences in business will be real consequences for the CEO.

- Don't wring your hands and whine. Don't blame and accuse. If your predecessor, or you, drove the car into a ditch, quickly get a tow truck and pull the car back onto the road.

- When making a decision it is okay to go with your highly tuned instinct, your gut (if you have resisted motivated reasoning), and ignore the roar of the mob. It is okay to go with the facts, if you understand the context. It is okay to blend your intuition with the rational side of your mind.

Jim Skinner (CEO, McDonald's): "Before deciding, get every point of view, especially from people who are unlike you, and who think differently than do you."

Larry Culp (CEO, Danaher Corp): "The best advice I ever received on decision making is to trust your gut. There is always an important place for homework, data, analysis, but the quest for perfect information, or the perfect answer can be endless and not necessarily optimal. I like to wallow in facts, inputs, but in the end, especially with tough calls, I go out for a run and keep running until the decision feels right. It's not what I was taught in business school, but my gut has served me well."

Be calm in crisis. Decide. Pull the trigger. Go to bed. Wake up. Review. If new facts, new information mean a change is necessary, then overrule yourself.

21

Plan with Principles

Bicron Corp. is a high-tech company that manufactures unique corona-free transformers valued for their exceptional long usage life in harsh environments. Chris Skomorowski, CEO, trained to buy and run an entrepreneurial company as CEO of a Fortune 1000 company. During its formative years, Bicron was entirely opportunistic. Bicron jumped on every doable sale opportunity that came its way without the guidance or discipline of a vision, a business plan, a company definition. Bicron operated five very different business models, with different profits and losses (P&L's), different inventory requirements, manufacturing operations, and sales channels.

Silos had sprung up. There were no job descriptions. People did jobs they liked. Cross-training did not exist.

There was uncertainty as to where the company made money. The inventory situation rivaled a museum's archives. The salesforce was thin. Many customers were serviced by inside customer service, and had never seen a Bicron person.

Bicron was a company picking up birdseed wearing boxing gloves. Chris Skomorowski took off the gloves.

Chris Skomorowski: "Bicron is a cool company. Management and workforce are excellent. The technology is astounding. We have transformers lying at the bottom of the ocean still working after 20 years. The company has shipped over a million parts, and not one has been defective. One high interest technology is what we call 'corona free.' 'Corona' is an electrical power by-product, a type of outgas that escapes from transformers and corrodes and destroys any electronics it encounters. 'Corona' is a major cost of failure in the electronics that run wind turbines and locomotives. Bicron is the only company that knows how to make corona-free components that never fail. And we have the most important asset in business: we have blue-chip, top-notch customers who are loyal and satisfied."

Chris Skomorowski: "We had to transform from a muddled organization, with too many loose ends, without a blueprint for intentional growth, to a managed, directed company. I communicated a set of management principles to the management team, and to everyone else. I asked everyone to think about the principles, what to add, how could we flesh out the principles so that they were relevant and directional. After everyone understood where I wanted Bicron to go, we did our homework, had a two-day retreat, crafted a transformation plan, and started changing the organization wherever we thought things could be improved. These principles guided our written transformation plan:

- Answer, 'What business are we in?'

- Identify the strategy for growth.

- Change is good. What must we change?

- Focus on product quality and delivery.

- Define our value proposition. Does our price reflect the value proposition?

- Identify everything we must improve. Prioritize projects and assign.

- Establish strict one-year and three-year improvement plans and review monthly.

- Create a culture of personal responsibility, that is truly customer oriented, where people are treated with respect and tolerance, and where everyone contributes to, and gets compensated for success.

- Invest in marketing and sales.

- Invest in innovation.

- Eliminate waste in everything we do: in the plants, in the labs, in the offices, in the field.

- Inventory is evil. Missing a delivery date is evil. Get the right mix.

- Better forecasting.

- Align the organization, the people, the job functions to the strategy.

- Listen to the employees. Act fast on good ideas. Let the recommenders implement when feasible.

- Spend company money as if it were your money.

- Reward and celebrate good performance and success.

- Continuous, open, honest, two-way communication with all stakeholders.

These are the principles we used to craft our transformation plan. These are the principles we are following to manage our transformation, and how we will manage in the future. We returned from our retreat and combined departments, changed reporting relationships, reprioritized our budgeting. Lots of change. Lots of positives."

Have principles. Have a plan. Work the plan.

22

"263 Is Zenny"

The average amount of training a new retail industry employee receives is seven to eight hours per year. The average turnover among retail industry employees is 120 percent a year. The average estimated cost of employee turnover is at least $40,000 per person per year. Out-of-pocket turnover costs include advertising the job, recruiting, interviewing, background checks, training, compensation, employee badges, compliance to a million government regulations.

Yet the biggest cost of turnover is invisible. The biggest cost of turnover is lost revenues. Sales are lost when the customer is ill served by an employee who knows little to nothing about the merchandise. Sales are lost when there are unmanned or undermanned departments or aisles or sections of the store. Sales are lost when a poorly trained sales person makes a mistake at the cash register. When a customer does not make a purchase, and leaves the store, that sale is lost forever.

At The Container Store, first-year, full-time employees receive 263 hours of training compared to the retail industry average. Employee turnover at The Container Store is less than 10 percent per year. That is 20 times lower than the retail average. This means The Container Store saves $1.7 million to $1.9 million per year in out-of-pocket turnover costs for every 100 employees it hires. It means The Container Store is generating at least $2 million more in sales per year, per every 100 employees than other companies competing for the same consumer's pocketbook.

> **Kip Tindell (CEO, The Container Store):** "I think employee training is the best investment we make. Every time we do a cost benefit analysis of our training investment, we conclude that it's worth taking training to the next level. To me, 263 hours is zenny."

The Container Store offers a solutions-based approach to retail, as opposed to selling individual products.

The company helps its customers save space, and ultimately, valuable time. Every employee is empowered to solve the customer's problems and to behave as if he or she were a store manager regardless of his or her role in the store.

> **Kip Tindell:** "One of our foundational principles is that one great person is equal to three good people. So, why not only hire great people? If you only hire great people, employees win because they get paid twice what other retailers would pay them. The company wins because it is getting three times the productivity at two times the payroll costs. The customer wins because she gets incredible service from passionate, well-trained employees. Our employees are furiously proud of their company, and they rarely leave. It is a winning strategy."

Now you know what Kip means when he claims that "263 is Zenny."

23

Dollarize or Die

"**D**ollarization" translates product benefits and claims into money; into the economic return the customer will receive after investing in the product. Dollarization guides marketers to price new products and application solutions to value, and not price to a target gross margin percentage, or to "meet the competition." Dollarization enables companies to reduce the risk of raising prices, and to get net positive price increases. Dollarization is an effective selling strategy to overcome the customer objection, "your price is too high." Dollarization is a tool to get customers to try the product, seek references about the product, and to ask for a product trial or demonstration. Dollarization safeguards innovation, creativity, research. Dollarization maximizes companies' returns on innovation and investment.

What does the customer know after she reads or hears that your product "lasts longer," "reduces energy costs," or is "more reliable"? The customer knows absolutely nothing. Nada. Zero. Zilch. All the customer knows is your price, and probably the price of all the other competing products. She does not know the facts, the proof of claim. She must be educated to the true dollarized value of your product in order to wisely decide.

Absent dollarization, the low price wins. Absent dollarization, the company loses the sale. Absent dollarization, all the thinking and engineering and marketing investments to commercialize the innovation are lost. The innovation dies, or never reaches its profit potential.

AN ACTUAL CASE STUDY

The customer requires a bearing for an air conditioning appliance his company sells to mobile home builders. He is evaluating two bearings that meet his technical specifications. One, a plain metal bearing, sells for $1.00, which is its major selling point. The second bearing sells for $4.00, and touts that it is "self-lubricating and longer lasting." The customer needs 100,000 bearings, which means there is a $300,000 price premium between the two bearings. The company gives a five-year warranty to his customers. The bearing customer sells to five mobile home builders. Which bearing should the customer buy?

DOLLARIZATION

The plain metal bearing depends on its low price to do the selling, and provides its price list and technical literature on the internet. The self-lubricating bearing company sends in a salesperson, a rainmaker, that rare breed of salespeople who dollarize and ring the cash register regardless of tough times. Using thoughtful questions, the rainmaker helps the customer to understand that at least 5 percent of the plain metal bearings will fail before 5 years pass, and that perhaps 1 to 2 percent of the lubricating bearings will fail. This means that a net 3 to 4 percent of bearings will fail before 5 years if they were to use the plain metal bearing. A net 4 percent means 4,000 warranty claims in 5 years. The average warranty cost is $400 in replacement parts, labor, downtime, travel. Thus, the $1.00 plain metal bearing actually costs $100,000 for the initial bearing purchase, plus $1,600,000 in warranty costs (4,000 claims × $400 per claim), for a total cost of $1,700,000.

The self-lubricating bearing will cost $400,000 for the initial bearing investment, plus up to $800,000 in warranty costs, for a total 5-year cost of $1,200,000. Thus, the net dollarized value of the self-lubricating bearing to the customer is at least $500,000, which does not include the cost of negative word-of-mouth, and the lost revenues when harmed mobile homebuilders switch air conditioning brands for their next purchase.

The rainmaker encourages the customer to do comparative failure tests on both bearings.

Rainmakers that sell premium-priced products know they must educate their customers to the total economic value of their product. They dollarize to overcome the eventual price objection, the customer's concern about the seller's higher price. Rainmakers don't sell products or services, technology or experience, features or benefits. They sell the dollarized value the customer gets from the product.

Rainmakers sell money. The bearing salesperson did not sell a self-lubricating bearing. He sold the economic value the air conditioner company received. He dollarized. He sold money. He sold $500,000.

Arunas Chesonis (CEO, PAETEC): "At PAETEC our salespeople show their customers how PAETEC can improve their companies. That improvement can be dollarized. The greater the dollarized value of our solution to our customers, the more money our salespeople make, the more money PAETEC makes, and the longer the economically driven relationship with our customers continues."

Dan Warmenhoven (Executive Chairman, NetApp): "No corporation wants to spend money on IT, on what we sell. They need IT, of course, but companies see that expense as overhead. So what we do at NetApp is to reduce our customers' overall cost of operations. One client, a large telecom, ran out of space and was facing an investment of $8 million to build a new data center. The NetApp solution was to modernize what they already had. We reduced their number of servers from 3,000 to 130, freeing up space, at $50–$100 per square foot, and saving on power. We saved them money in every category. We eliminated 8,000 switch ports, two megawatts of power. The dollarized value of their savings is over $1 million a year, plus they did not have to spend $8 million on a new data center. If their cost of capital is 15 percent, NetApp saved them another $1.2 million a year."

Chris Jones (CEO, Microcare Corp.): "We sell premium products at premium prices. We have to dollarize. For example, one of our products is priced two times higher than the competition's, about $40 per unit. We help our customers calculate the true cost, the actual quantitative, mathematical value, of our higher priced product. Microcare cleans 100 percent of their parts, 100 percent clean, 100 percent of the time. The other guys only clean 70 percent of the parts. What does it cost the customer to reclean 30 percent of his parts? What does it cost to ship a dirty part and get it back? Our "higher price" is always the lowest cost."

There is always someone who will offer a product seemingly like yours for a lower price. If you don't dollarize your value proposition you will unnecessarily lose sales. If you depend on adages such as "reduce fuel consumption," to sell your product you will lose to the company that says, "ABC Widgets reduce fuel consumption by one gallon a day, saving you $900 a year."

Lose too many sales and the product dies.

Dollarize or die.

Always Price to Value

When it comes to pricing a product or service, it doesn't matter what it costs to make the product or provide the service. If you make a product for $.10 and it is worth $1.00, then the price should be $1.00. If it costs $2.00 to make a product, and its value is $1.99, then drop the product. If the $1.99 product is new, don't introduce.

The single most important driver of profitability is price. On average, a 1 percent net increase in price raises net operating profits by 10 to 12 percent. A 1 percent cut in price reduces profitability by 7 to 9 percent. Thus, if you raise the price of a product that sells for $100 to $101, you raise net profits by approximately 11 percent.

If your product sells for $1.00, and the salesperson begs you to cut the price to $.99—"It's only a penny!"—and you cave in, you will reduce net operating profits by 8 percent. (Run the numbers on your product line to determine the impact of price on your bottom line.)

Pricing to value means the marketer must know the dollarized value of the product to the customer. The marketer must know the true value of the competitors' offerings. The marketer must know which segment of the marketplace can pay for the innovation or unique product points of difference.

> **Ayn LaPlant (CEO, Beekley Corp.):** "Our first mammography marker was the size of a BB. Customers said they would pay 1 cent for the product. But we knew the marker's value. It saved radiologists time. It reduced the number of 'return for rescreening' calls that women, and their families, dread. It improved radiologists diagnoses. And our Beekley Medical product would save lives by enabling early detection of a cancer or a potential cancer. We priced that marker for $1.00, a hundred times higher than what our research suggested. We price to value."

Arunas Chesonis (CEO, PAETEC): "We decided early on that PAETEC would be a national provider, but focused on a niche where we could provide tangible value, with a product line priced to reflect that value. Our target segment is large- and medium-size business clients. We do business with 46,000 companies in 85 of the top 100 geographical markets in the United States. Our targeted niche/price-to-value strategy is working. In 10 years revenues grew from zero dollars to $2 billion."

Charles Lanktree (CEO, Eggland's Best): "Eggland's Best made a better, healthier egg. We figured consumers put a high value on their health. We have the highest cost of content. Better product. Higher price. Better value. Consumers feel our price premium is worth it, as we grow double-digits every month. Our retailers love EB's pricing. They make considerably more money on an EB dozen than they do on other eggs. Because we are growing, the stores turn EB eggs faster, adding to their profits. Store managers tell me that EB is one of their most profitable items. Our farmers make more money. By pricing to the value of our innovation—a better egg—every stakeholder is enriched."

When setting price consider whether your product is enabling. If your product uniquely enables a customer to do something such as eliminate a maintenance problem, your product is worth a percentage of what it would cost the customer to do the repair. If your product eliminates hydraulic oil leakage, your product is worth a percentage of the value of the oil saved. If your prouct makes it possible for a customer to improve his product, which leads to greater revenues for the customer, your product should be priced to reflect some of that additional revenue.

Calculate the economic consequences for your customers the money they will lose if they go without your product or service. That consequence is your product's dollarized value and should be priced to reflect that value.

Price to value and increase profits.

25

Sell. Sell. Sell.

The transformative CEO knows that the company will do what he or she does. The transformative CEO knows that getting and keeping profitable customers is the most worthy of marketing missions. The transformative CEO wants every employee riveted to serving the customer, and wants every employee to be tied directly or indirectly to driving revenues. So the transformative CEO visits customers, makes sales calls on prospects, meets with salespeople, sits in the front row during sales meetings.

Pat McGovern (Founder and Chairman, International Data Group[IDG]): "Get out there and talk to potential buyers of your products and services to make sure that there is a need that you can really fulfill. If you find a good need to fulfill, the rest will come about naturally."

Joseph Taylor (CEO, Panasonic North America): "In my first 100 days as CEO, I virtually lived on an airplane. I visited all our top customers; all our channel partners; and all our major suppliers, as I expect our suppliers to sell for us because they sell to us and we do business with them. I met hundreds of people as I crisscrossed the country. I learned what our customers like and dislike about Panasonic, and what they want going forward. I am confident that every Panasonic employee knows that I care about our customers."

AJ Khubani (Founder; CEO, TeleBrands): "I wanted to sell our products in retail stores, not just on television. This meant getting retailers to buy and promote the products. Of course, I started by calling on the biggest retail stores first. Complete rejection. Got nowhere. The buyers wouldn't talk to me. I couldn't even get a guy to answer the phone. I heard 'no' in one form or another, at least 50 times. But I was persistent because I knew our products would sell in stores and make retailers a lot of money. Finally, I got an appointment with a small retailer in New Jersey, then called Herman Sporting Goods. The guy had strong objections to selling my AmberVision sunglasses. 'You are a one-product company. Your packaging is ugly. You sell directly to consumers. We sell directly to consumers. You are a competitor. You know nothing about selling at retail stores.' I looked at the guy and said, 'You are correct, I know nothing about retail, but you do. If you were selling my sunglasses, we wouldn't be competitors, we would be partners. Why don't you take advantage of the huge brand awareness our TV commercials have created, and give it a try? Why don't you do a test with a thousand pairs?' And then I waited and waited for him to answer. Reluctantly, he finally croaked, 'We'll take 600 pairs and if they don't sell they're going back.' In the first week, Herman sold 300 pairs, an unbelievable 50 percent sell through. And we were on our way selling in retail stores. Herman's 'yes' trumped 50 'nos.'"

Chris Jones (CEO, Microcare Corp.): "I may be CEO, but I am actually a salesman. I inherited a Rolodex of customers and prospects from my father, who was a manufacturer's rep and a super salesman. Microcare is now an international company. My job is to promote innovation in everything we do, including new products, and to be sure we never stop calling on customers, always listening to customers, and never stop selling. I think of my second-in-command as our head of sales. Our president of Microcare Asia is a salesman. Our VP of R&D is a salesman. He has to talk to customers to find out what they need. Our VP, human assets sells. She sells talent on coming to work for us. Our director of marketing is a salesperson. She sells our distributors, our customers. When a customer visits one of our plants, I expect every single employee in that plant to welcome the customer, and to sell or resell that customer by offering the hospitality of Microcare."

The transformative CEO believes that if the customer doesn't do business with his or her company, then both lose. Transformative CEOs do not like to lose. They are always selling.

Never stop selling. Hire rainmakers.

Continually train your rainmakers and your sales managers to improve selling efficiency (face time with customers) and selling effectiveness (closing the sale with fewer sales calls).

26

Be a Bold Brand Builder

rand names are often the most valuable assets a company owns. The brand names Coke and Coca-Cola are worth more than all the plants and equipment and bottlers the Coca-Cola Company owns. Consumer package goods companies have always known the value of brands. Business-to-business marketers are starting to understand the economic leverage and advantage that strong brand names command.

Brands are a promise. (For example, Honest Tea's, "Real Tea. Real Taste. Honest." Or Campbell Soup's, "M'mm M'mm Good. M'mm M'mm Good. That's what Campbell Soups are: M'mm M'mm good.") When the brand owner delivers on the promise, the brand owner gets loyal customers, positive word of mouth, and reduced marketing costs to acquire new customers.

Strong brands usually have leading market shares. Brands with high shares in their target market segments are often the most profitable. Positive brand awareness can earn a 7 percent price premium, based solely on the brand name.

> **Shelly Lazarus (Chairman, Ogilvy & Mather):** "The primary marketing effort is to build brands. Brands drive sales, and capture market share. There are countless ways to build a brand: the way the package looks; the way the phone is answered; the way customer complaints are handled; the way the store and showroom looks; the way delivery trucks look and are driven. Any company's biggest brand advocates are the people who work in the company. They are the proselytizers. They wear the uniform, the baseball cap with the company logo. The people in a company can be the embodiment of the brand. Too often leaders don't pay attention to the internal audience. However, the transformative CEO completely understands these interwoven brand dynamics."

Dan Amos (CEO, Aflac): "One of the main jobs of the CEO is to build and protect the brand. In part, that means anyone connected to Aflac is part of our brand. Thus, our employees and agents must always behave appropriately and be extremely ethical. I do not put up with anything that would in any way tarnish our brand, the image of the company."

Daniel Lamarre (CEO, Cirque du Soleil): "Our brand is our shows that are stunningly creative. When we protect our show creators, we are protecting our brand. We are always monitoring our customers: what they think of our brand; how they perceive it; and what their expectations are from our brand."

Seth Goldman (CEO, Honest Tea): "We wanted to create a brand that meant something to people. We created a brand that stands for health, holistic living, for the betterment of society and the environment. Our brand name is 'Honest'. Our ethos is honesty."

Jim McCann (CEO, 1-800-Flowers): "Our brand is also our telephone number, our Internet address, and our promise of delivering a smile for our customers, even when they order at the last possible minute. We need to be vigilant when it comes to our brand—how we behave in all aspects of our business and with all of our constituencies."

Joe Grano (Former CEO, UBS Paine Webber; CEO, Centurion Holdings LLC and Producer of *Jersey Boys*): "I don't have to worry if the cast of *Jersey Boys*' will ever deliver a sub-par show. The show is about them! The songs and music and story comprise the show's brand promise. The audience is never failed."

Brands build revenues. Brands build equity. Brands are assets. Good brands outlive management. Good brands span generations. Build big brands. Build brands boldly. Build your business.

27

Tell Stories

Many people more vividly remember lessons learned from hearing or reading stories than they do from studying dusty textbooks. Before Johannes Gutenberg's transformative printing press (1455), humans maintained their cultures, and educated their children, by telling stories (and making art). The storyteller and the poet were celebrities of the oral tradition. Books and scrolls and parchments were rare and expensive. It is not surprising that Guttenberg's first "mass-produced" book was the Bible, itself a collection of stories.

The Ritz-Carlton Hotel expects all employees to do whatever it takes to make the guest's experience so memorable, so satisfying, that the guest will come back, and will tell others to visit. This expectation is at the core of the Ritz-Carlton's "guest satisfaction above all" culture. To maintain this culture, to keep it front of the mind and to better communicate what is expected of its ladies and gentlemen, the Ritz-Carlton tells stories. The Ritz-Carlton tells "Wow Stories."

Every Monday and every Friday, every week of the year, in every Ritz-Carlton around the world, employees gather to share "Wow Stories." "Wow Stories" communicate, train and illustrate the Ritz-Carlton's overriding ethic to care for its guests.

> **Simon Cooper (Former President, Ritz-Carlton):** "'Wow Stories' are about the great things our ladies and gentlemen have done. I love our 'Wow Stories.' They recognize standout people. More important, they introduce or remind everybody of the kinds of service behaviors that we endorse and that bring our customers back again and again."

> **Simon Cooper:** "Our 'Wow Stories' are amazing. About once or twice a month a well-trained Ritz-Carlton security officer saves a guest's life somewhere in the world. A waiter in the Dubai Ritz overheard a gentleman and his wife, who was in a wheelchair, musing at

dinner that it was a pity he could not get his wife to the beach for a sunset dinner. The waiter told maintenance. Maintenance told the Food and Beverage Manager. Everybody met and by the next evening there was a wooden walkway to the beach ending at a private tent with a dinner table set for two. The wait-staff in attendance included people to help get the lady's wheelchair to the tent. A candle-lit dinner for two on the beach of Dubai. That's a 'wow'. How many potential guests do you think that couple have steered to the Ritz-Carlton?"

1-800-Flowers is famous for exceptional customer service. 1-800-Flowers not only delivers on time on Valentine's Day, Secretary's Day, and Mother's Day, they also help say "Happy Birthday" to 380,000 people every day of the year. Jim McCann is the founder and CEO of 1-800-Flowers.

Jim McCann: "In addition to developing programs to teach our new people what we mean by having a 'caring team, obsessed with service,' we are also continuously training our veterans, always remembering to set goals, measure and reward performance. One of our best teaching tools is our 'Book of Legends.' Our 'Book of Legends' is a set of ever-growing volumes filled with letters we have received from customers thanking one of our people for extraordinary customer service. These letters are real life examples of what we expect, love and reward. We also ask our people to write their customer engagement stories for another book we keep. If one of our people feels happy, inspired by something he or she has done for a customer, he or she is encouraged to write a letter to me. Every letter is read and gets a response. Our 'Books of Legends' are themselves legendary in our company."

The best story telling company in the world is probably the largest organization that few have heard of. Sodexo Health Care has $3.2 billion in revenues and 65,000 employees. It is a division of Sodexo, Inc., headquartered in Paris, which has an additional 130,000 employees around the world. Sodexo Health Care prepares and serves the food, and manages facilities for hospitals, schools, universities, nursing homes, and retirement communities. And Pat Connolly, president of Sodexo Health Care knows the value of stories.

Pat Connolly: "Sodexo offers quality of life services. We are unwaveringly committed to improving the quality of life of the patients in hospitals, the elderly in a nursing home, and everyone else we touch. We see the patients as our customers, not the hospital that pays us. My job is to insure that every one of my 65,000 colleagues is completely connected to the quality of life of the customers they see every day. The way I maintain and promote our quality of life connection is by telling stories."

Pat Connolly: "I'm not big on hierarchy and multi-layered management. I have open forums all year long where I visit with our people who touch and serve and talk to our customers. The forums usually have 15 people. I show up. No entourage. I tell stories of colleagues' outstanding performances. I listen to their concerns and ideas for improving our services, our company. I directly answer any question. Every employee, regardless of her job, can call me with issues, without fear of consequences. Some of our best ideas come from these calls."

Not only does Pat Connolly tell stories, he collects them. He encourages employees and managers to send him stories. He receives approximately 350 stories a month. At the end of the year, the five or six most amazing stories are celebrated at an annual meeting. The employee and his or her spouse are VIPs of that meeting. "I love to tell those stories, and to share hundreds of other stories throughout the company." Pat Connolly said.

Pat Connolly: "Let me tell you some Sodexo stories that illustrate our culture. There is an elderly gentleman in a nursing home who is no longer able to do what he loved to do, and that was to drive every Sunday to his favorite ice cream store. So now, every Sunday, our people go to that store and get him ice cream. Better quality of life."

"A retirement community has a weekly buffet night, which the residents love. Some of the folks are no longer able to easily walk the line, load trays, and safely get back to their dining table. So we introduced a 'rolling buffet'. We roll the buffet to the table, to our customers. They can make choices. They can participate without an accident. We gave them back dignity. We rolled out that 'rolling buffet' idea across the country."

"A little kid was in a hospital recovering from an operation. Somehow she lost her teddy bear. We looked everywhere. No luck. We own 26 huge laundry plants that clean and supply linens and uniforms to hospitals. Our housekeeper had the idea that maybe, perhaps, the teddy bear might have been hidden in the change of linen. She called the manager of our laundry plant. The manager and his colleagues spent hours looking though hundreds of thousands of pounds of sheets and pillowcases. They found the teddy bear, stitched it, cleaned it, and returned it to our little kid. Our compensation? Just a smile."

Pat Connolly: "When the tornadoes brutalized Joplin, Missouri, Sodexo employees jumped into cars and trucks, all volunteers, drove to Joplin and did what we do best. Gave assistance and improved peoples' quality of life.

"That famous story of trucks full of bottled water getting to New Orleans after Hurricane Katrina? That's a Sodexo story."

Legh Knowles CEO (retired) of Beaulieu Vineyard in Napa Valley was famous for his stories of BV wines being served at the White House, as gifts to kings and queens, as the favorite's of Joe DiMaggio and Marilyn Monroe. "If I don't tell the stories of Beaulieu," Legh Knowles said, "You can bet our competitors won't either."

Tell stories. People like stories. Your people love to be in your stories. People remember stories.

28

Beware of Your To-Do List

There is always some sense of satisfaction when you draw a line through some task on your to-do list. That's one reason to-do lists are addictive to the busy manager. But to-do lists are not proxies for performance. That you crossed off 20 things on your to-do list doesn't mean you got anything important done. Short lists are good. Checklists are often job critical, such as preflight and presurgery protocols. Important projects, listed democratically with 50 other items on a typical to-do list, don't get done. "Short" means a list of three to eight top priority projects. Working on too many things means little gets finished, or finished well. Working on the wrong things is a total waste.

Steve Jobs (CEO, Apple) only worked on six to eight projects at a time. His list included such mundane initiatives as, create the Mac, launch iPhone, launch iPad, open Apple Stores, launch iTunes and transform the music industry. The only Top 10 List Steve Jobs ever had was on his iPod.

Calin Rovinescu was named CEO of Air Canada on April Fools' Day, 2009. The company was on the brink of bankruptcy. Thirteen months later, Air Canada was named the number one airline in North America. Air Canada flies to 175 destinations, has 26,000 employees, 29,000 retirees, and carries 33 million customers a year. Despite such complexity, and despite the desparate condition of Air Canada when Mr. Rovinescu joined as CEO, he had only four items on his to-do list.

> **Calin Rovinescu:** "With the size of our company, four priorities doesn't sound like a lot, but I wanted the entire organization, every person, to focus on just four things."

Calin Rovinescu's to-do list:

1. Take $500 million in costs out of the company without cutting employee wages or benefits.

2. Re-engage with the customer.

3. Exploit the Air Canada brand in international markets.

4. Change the culture from a government-owned mentality to a more nimble entrepreneurial company.

> **Anne Mulcahy (CEO, Xerox, now Chairperson of Save the Children):** "Someone once gave me good advice. He told me not to have more than three objectives. That doesn't mean there aren't a lot of other things going on in big, complex global companies. But when you want people to focus, you have to give priorities that they can manage. Three."

It takes clear-eyed objectivity to select the correct three to eight projects. Each project must be essential to changing and growing the business. Each project must be tethered to the central core purpose of the organization. It takes mental toughness not to chase the glamorous; to put off the aggressive board member's new product idea; to pass on that key "never-be-a-better-time" acquisition.

Only work on three to eight top priority projects.

Beware of your diverting to-do list. Keep a short list in your pocket. Your list must be indelible: in your mind, and in the mind of every person in the organization.

29

80 Percent Is a Lot

"**G**etting it all" is not a worthy mission. Getting it all may sound like a rallying cry, but it is not realistic, almost never achieved, and never worth the marginal cost of the last few points. Getting it all is aggressive, macho, tough talk, and all that jazz, but is an unsound goal or management principle.

Achieving 80 percent of a negotiation goal, 80 percent of a cost reduction goal, 80 percent of a market share goal, is rarely a losing outcome. To illustrate, sales managers and compensation people are constantly trying to craft a perfect salesforce compensation plan. But when there is more than one person participating in the compensation plan, the plan will be imperfect. There will always be concerns about who made the sale, or who contributed to making the sale. There will be yakkity-yak about commission splits, account ownership, differences in territory potential, and on and on and on, as salespeople are expert at peeling, coring, and slicing compensation plans. Shoot for a 100 percent perfect compensation plan, but settle for 80 to 90 percent. After you get the 80 percent, then deal with the outlier issues.

> **Calin Rovinescu (CEO, Air Canada):** "Too many people want to take the last nickel off the table. They want to have 100 percent success. My version of the 80/20 rule is that 'if I get 80 percent of what I wanted, I'll be happy. If I get 80 percent of what I want in a labor negotiation, that will probably be a good deal.'"

> **Dick Pechter (CEO, Pershing, Retired):** "One key to getting a successful, lasting negotiated deal is to leave some money on the table for the other guy. You may be able to get the last penny. You may deserve that last penny. But that last penny is not worth it."

Ken O'Keefe is the offensive coach and quarterback coach for the University of Iowa football team. He tells his quarterbacks that they don't have to get a touchdown on every play. They should act like a business person and try "to make a little profit on every play."

Getting 80 percent of a lot of negotiations adds up to a winning score.

Andrew Carnegie was on his deathbed. He was asked, "You are the most famous industrialist of all time. What is the secret to your success? Do you have a lesson for posterity?"

Andrew Carnegie answered, "Fill the other guy's basket to the brim, then making money becomes an easy proposition."

30

A $700 Billion
Cost Cut

Henry Kaiser was one of the greatest builders in the United States. He built bridges, dams, waterways. He was the number one builder of ships in WWII. He was foresighted and enlightened when it came to the health care of his company's thousands of employees. Keeping workers working, healthy, on the job, is smart business. A worker who is worried about a sick child is not as productive as normal. Reducing the amount of health care money paid to retirees lowers costs, making companies more competitive. Kaiser built another permanent structure, named Kaiser Permanente. Kaiser Permanente was, and is, a group of clinics and hospitals, staffed by teams of physicians and nurses, that delivers preventive health care, as well as treatment of illness and pain.

The medical team concept was new and novel in the 1940s, and it is new and novel today. Kaiser Permanente is a health care delivery organization with 36 hospitals, nearly 9 million members, about 180,000 employees with more than $47 billion in revenues. George Halvorson is CEO.

George Halvorson: "Henry Kaiser was truly transformative. My job is to keep transforming, to keep adapting to changing needs and regulations, to keep the Kaiser culture responsive and dedicated to our mission."

George Halvorson: "Every year the United States spends $2.7 trillion on health care, and the amount is growing. I am convinced that the Kaiser model, combined with other proven cost-reducing best practices, could reduce that annual cost by $700 billion, the equivalent of the so-called 'stimulus plan.' Today the health care industry's compensation system, how providers get paid, is perversely designed to create financial rewards built around bad options for the patient.

There is almost nothing in the system to financially incentivize doctors to do a better job preventing heart attacks, preventing kidney failures, preventing strokes. Unhealthy patients generate the revenues. 75 percent of the cost of care in America goes to patients with chronic conditions. 80 percent of the cost of health care is spent on 10 percent of the patients.

"Prevention is the big cost reduction opportunity."

George Halvorson: "Diabetes is the fastest growing disease in America. 32 percent of the entire cost of Medicare goes to patients who are diabetic. Diabetes is essentially preventable. And only 8 percent of diabetics are diagnosed early enough to prevent very high cost issues such as kidney failure. Increase that preventive diagnosis to 80 percent and we would cut the number of kidney failures by 50 percent. That is one of many fixable scenarios.

Here is a specific example of how the Kaiser Permanente concept of medical teams cuts costs: We set a goal of reducing by half the number of our senior patients who suffer broken bones. We identified the high-risk patients, implemented our team care approach, resulting in an outcome of 47 percent fewer broken bones. Prevention is big money."

Henry Kaiser knew that preventing illness reduced costs, the cost of care, and that the same prevention increased revenues, by increasing worker productivity.

$7 billion a year is serious money.

31

Look to the Numbers

The transformative CEOs expect their companies, as compared to ordinary companies, to overinvest in servicing customers; to overinvest in hiring; overinvest in training; overinvest in all elements of their winning strategies. Some illuminating numbers:

1. **45,000** The number of quality tests Eggland's Best conducts each year as compared to the 300 to 400 tests conducted by all other egg producers combined. Charlie Lanktree is CEO.

2. **47** The percentage of high-risk patients who do not suffer broken bones because they are members of Kaiser Permanente; and benefit from Kaiser's innovative health care protocols. George Halvorson is CEO.

3. **70** The percentage of days per year Lynn Tilton, CEO Patriarch Partners, travels to customers and owned companies. Patriarch has saved over 250,000 American jobs.

4. **60,000** The number of employees AT&T Mobility merged in just 19 days. Ralph de la Vega is CEO of AT&T Mobility.

5. **12,371** The number of people who auditioned to be the new voice of the Aflac Duck, a publicity coup. Dan Amos is CEO.

6. **2** The percentage of job applicants that are eventually hired by the Ritz-Carlton. Simon Cooper is former president.

7. **1,000s** The number of General Mills employees that volunteer significant time to others and their communities. Ken Powell is CEO.

8. **3,000** The number of extraordinary customer "bettering life" stories Sodexo Health Care employees submit, share, and celebrate each year. Pat Connolly is president.

9. **263** The number of training hours each Container Store employee receives in their first year on the job

as compared to the retail industry average of 7 to 8 hours. Kip Tindell is CEO.

10. **70,000,000** The number of girls who have made the Girl Scout Promise since 1912. Kathy Cloninger is the former Girl Scout CEO.

32

Live and Lead by the Girl Scout Law

The Girl Scouts are more than cookies and camp. The Girl Scouts produce good citizens, responsible adults, and leaders. The Girl Scouts help girls reach their highest potential. For over 100 years, The Girl Scouts have transformed the notion that leadership is a male-only province. Since its founding in 1912 nearly 70 million girls have been Girl Scouts. Nearly 70 percent of today's women leaders in the United States, in civic organizations, business, politics, and education, were Girl Scouts. Every woman astronaut was a Girl Scout. Approximately 50 Girl Scouts are regularly elected to the House of Representatives and the U.S. Senate. Ten Girl Scouts have won Olympic Gold Medals. The Girl Scouts create leaders.

LEADERS INCLUDING:

Madeleine Albright—Former U.S. Secretary of State

Jacqueline Allison—Rear Admiral/Navy

Melissa Sue Anderson—Actress ("Little House on the Prairie")

Lucille Ball—Comedienne

Candace Bergen—Actress

Polly Bergen—Actress

Amelia Betanzos—President/CEO, Wildcat Service Corp

Shirley Temple Black—Actress and U.S. Ambassador to the United Nations

Bonnie Blair—1994 Gold Medal Olympian Figure Skater

Erma Bombeck—Author

Rita Braver—Correspondent, "CBS News"

Dr. Joyce Brothers—Psychologist; Radio and
Television Personality

Laura Bush—Wife of President George W. Bush,
(43rd President). She is also the Honorary President
of Girls Scouts, USA

Mariah Carey—Singer

Lynda Carter—Actress

Rosalyn Carter—Wife of President Jimmy Carter
(39th President)

Peggy Cass—Actress

Suzy Chaffee—Skier; World Freestyle Skiing
Champion, 1971–1973

Chelsea Clinton—Daughter of Bill Clinton
(42nd President)

Hillary Rodham Clinton—U.S. Senator and Wife
of Bill Clinton (42nd President)

Susan Collins—U.S. Senator from Maine

Katie Couric—News Anchorwoman

Betty Davis—Actress

Sandra Day O'Connor—Associate Justice, U.S. Supreme Court

Celine Dion—Singer

Elizabeth Dole—Former President, American Red Cross

Elizabeth II—Queen of England

Carol C. Elliott—Brigadier General, USAF

Geraldine Ferraro—Former House Representative for New York and Vice Presidential Candidate

Debbi Fields—Mrs. Fields Cookies Founder

Peggy Fleming—1968 Figure Skating Gold Medal Olympian

Tipper Gore—Wife of Former Vice President Al Gore

Ella Grasso—Former Governor of Connecticut

Florence Griffith-Joyner—Olympic Gold Medalist; Track and Field Athlete

Dorothy Hamill—1976 Figure Skating Gold Medal Olympian

Helen Hayes—Actress

Ricki Tigert Heifer—Former Chair, Federal Deposit Insurance Corp.

Lou Henry Hoover—Wife of President Herbert Hoover (31st President)

Nancy Kassenbaum—U.S. Senator from Kansas

Grace Kelly—Actress

Ethel Kennedy—Wife of Robert Kennedy (Presidential Candidate)

Jeanne Kirkpatrick—Former U.S. Ambassador to the United Nations

Dorothy Lamour—Actress

Ann Landers—Advice Columnist

Rebecca Lobo—WNBA Basketball Player

Nancy Lopez—Pro Golfer

Susan Lucci—Actress

Ellen Marram—Former President, Tropicana

Natalie Merchant—Singer

Barbara Mikulski—U.S. Senator from Maryland

Ann Moore—Publisher, *People* magazine

Erin Moriarty—TV Reporter, CBS "48 Hours"

Pat Nixon—Wife of President Richard Nixon (37th President)

Julie Nixon Eisenhower—Daughter of Richard Nixon (37th President)

Dolly Parton—Singer

Jane Pauley—TV Reporter, "Dateline"

Princess Anne—Olympian and President of Save the Children

Princess Margaret—Princess of England, Charity Worker

Nancy Reagan—Wife of President Ronald Reagan (40th President)

Janet Reno—Former U.S. Attorney General

Debbie Reynolds—Actress

Dr. Sally Ride—Astronaut, First U.S. Woman in Space

Cathy Rigby—Olympic Gymnast and Television Commentator

Pat Schroeder—First Female Congressional Representative from Colorado

Helen Sharman—First British Woman in Space

Claire Shipman—White House Correspondent, "NBC News"

Dinah Shore—Actress

Gloria Steinem—Author

Martha Stewart—Television personality

Taylor Swift—Singer

Marlo Thomas—Actress

Cheryl Tiegs—Model

Mary Tyler Moore—Actress

Barbara Walters—Anchorwoman of ABC's "20/20" and "The View"

Dionne Warwick—Singer

Elizabeth Watson—Houston Police Chief

Sheila Widnall—U.S. Secretary of the Air Force (Retired)

Venus Williams—Tennis Pro

General Myrna Williamson—Retired Army General

Judy Woodruff—Anchor and Senior Correspondent, "CNN"

Kathy Cloninger (CEO, Girl Scouts of the USA) emphasizes, "We are really about leadership in this country. We are building girls who grow up to be courageous and confident, who have the right kind of character, who are grounded in the Girl Scout Law, and who then go on to make America a better place. Our brand is about citizen leadership. We tell our girls you don't have to wait until you are an adult to be a leader."

Transformative leaders understand what the Girl Scouts mean by teaching confidence and courage.

> **Kathy Cloninger:** "Leadership is about self-confidence. In the Girl Scouts, girls and volunteers try lots of things, fail at some, succeed at many. We teach girls to have the courage to stand up to peers. To not succumb to peer pressure, to do the right thing when everybody else is going in a different direction."

One of the most incredible marketing successes in all of commerce is the Girl Scout Cookies phenomenon. The Cookie Sale teaches girls financial entrepreneurship, selling skills, and ethical business practices.

> **Kathy Cloninger:** "The Girls Scouts Cookie Sale, and thousands of lesser known activities, give our girls practical, hands-on training that is purposeful experience for future leaders."

THE GIRL SCOUT PROMISE AND LAW:

The Girl Scout Promise and Law are shared by every member of Girl Scouting. The Girl Scout Promise is the way Girl Scouts agree to act every day toward one another and to other people, and the Girl Scout Law outlines a way to act toward one another and the world.

Girl Scout Promise

On my honor, I will try:
To serve God and my country,
To help people at all times,
And to live by the Girl Scout Law.

Girl Scout Law

I will do my best to be
Honest and fair,
Friendly and helpful,
Considerate and caring,
Courageous and strong, and
Responsible for what I say and do,
And to
Respect myself and others,
Respect authority, use resources wisely,
Make the world a better place, and
Be a sister to every Girl Scout.

Live and lead by the Girl Scout Law.

33

Exude Delight

Customers are people. Employees are people. Suppliers are people. When a person connected to your enterprise does anything that helps the enterprise, exude delight. People want to be recognized, appreciated, and thanked. Genuine, happy, warm thank-yous never hurt.

When any teacher in the school gives a certain three-year-old pupil anything, even just a lollipop, she responds with a huge smile, claps her hands, and squeals, "For me?" The three-year old exudes delight. The teacher is thrilled, touched. That little girl is every teacher's pet.

When a customer makes a purchase, exude delight. When a customer gives positive word-of-mouth, gives a referral, makes a suggestion, voices a complaint, exude delight.

When a coworker solves a problem, makes a sale, lends a hand, packs a box, empties the trash, delivers a product, exude delight. When the UPS guy delivers, exude delight.

> **Ayn LaPlant (CEO, Beekley Corp.):** "When I hear spontaneous cheering and clapping, I know we are having another wonderful day."

Exude delight and build loyalties. It costs nothing.

Epilogue

Fun

Turning around companies, founding companies, transforming cultures, industries, societies is tough day labor. Despite the toil, Transformative CEOs have fun and put fun into business. Mark Dixon, CEO Regus, keeps a wind surfing board ready to catch the next big wave. Jim McCann, Founder and CEO 1-800-Flowers "delivers smiles." Tony Hsieh, CEO Zappos, "delivers happiness." Larry Culp's mantra at Danaher Corp., (he is CEO) is "winning is fun." Danaher has lots of fun. Jim Skinner (CEO, McDonald's) sells millions of "Happy Meals" every week.

Maxine Clark (CEO, Build-A-Bear Workshop): "Any successful business runs on fun, and what could be more fun than building your own teddy bear?"

Lots of fun. But Joe Grano (Former Chairman and CEO of UBS PaineWebber, now CEO, Centurion Holdings, LLC) wins the fun game. He has excellent seats, and backstage passes, show time, any time, to the massive Broadway hit, *Jersey Boys*. *Jersey Boys* is based on the hit music of Frankie Valli and Bob Gaudio of The Four Seasons (all members of the Rock and Roll Hall of Fame). Joe Grano has been friends with Frankie Valli and Bob Gaudio for over 30 years. After all the traditional Broadway investors said "no" to backing the musical, Joe Grano, customarily, said, "why not." Since the show opened, over 12 million people worldwide have seen *Jersey Boys*.

From the incomparable Bob Gaudio, the lyrics from his "Big Man in Town":

> *"Money, I don't have any,*
> *I'm down to my last penny*
> *I'm gonna make it,*
> *Just wait and see."*

Transformative CEOs make it. Have fun everybody.

Index

About the Authors

Jeffrey Fox is the founder of Fox & Company, Inc in Chester, CT, a consulting firm that works with companies to increase their revenues and gross profit margins. He has written twelve international best selling books. There are over 200 international editions of his books. Jeffrey's books, including "How to Become a CEO," have been *New York Times*, *Wall Street Journal*, and *BusinessWeek* best sellers. His books are best sellers in Russia, Singapore, Turkey, and Hong Kong. Four of Jeffrey's books have been number one in France. He was a Capital Area Scholar at Trinity College, where he was also named "Person of the Year." He has an MBA from Harvard Business School.

Robert Reiss is founder and host of *The CEO Show*, nationally syndicated to more than 600,000 listeners on AM/FM radio. His company publishes *The CEO Forum*, a quarterly magazine whose subscription base is exclusively 10,000 CEOs. Reiss is a frequent keynote speaker on lessons from CEOs.

He is a regular contributor with *Forbes.com,* where he has written over 30 columns on CEO perspective. His work with CEOs was featured in the *Harvard Business Review,* where Reiss was cited as an "expert in executive communications."

In 2011 Reiss launched *The CEO TV Show* which is the first pan mobile program featuring CEOs who have reinvented the fabric of American industry. Reiss is also chairman of The Conference Board's Annual Senior Marketing Executive Conference, which in 2009 was cited in Weber Shandwick's annual research as the number four Global C-Suite Conference.

His not-for-profit work includes being a Trustee for Kingsbrook Medical Center and a Director at Griffin Health Services Corporation (*Fortune* magazine's fourth best company to work for in America, 2006) and a director for Planetree. In 2008, Reiss was recipient of The United Hospital Fund's *Distinguished Trustee Award*.